the
Warrior
Method

SEBASTIAN BATES

R3THINK PRESS

First published in Great Britain 2018
by Rethink Press (www.rethinkpress.com)

Praise

'Educators like Sebastian are a breath of fresh air and a true rarity. His systematic and holistic approach to developing the character of young people has without a doubt transformed thousands of lives. In this wonderful and valuable book for both parents and the martial arts community, he shares his insights and powerful Warrior methodology.'
— Steven Shove
Co-founder, Really Wild Education

'Every parent wants their child to be confident, happy and live a life filled with opportunity. In *The Warrior Method* Sebastian has fused together an approach, borrowed from ancient wisdom, to address modern pressures – one made even more compelling when he was forced to apply it to a crisis in his own life with extraordinary results. A remarkable story of recovery and personal triumph. Living proof that this method can give you the confidence to overcome anything.'
— Sara Milne Row
Founder/Owner of Coaching Impact Limited

To our incredible Black Belt Community of Instructors, staff, parents, ambassadors and students - past, present and future. You inspire me.

Contents

Introduction

The single biggest challenge parents face is ensuring their child develops into a happy, successful and ambitious adult. And this is an even bigger challenge when parents are managing their own typically stressful, modern lifestyle.

Do you find yourself asking:

- How can I reduce my stress levels and have more quality family time?

- How can I teach my child about respect and improve their behaviour effectively?

Modern parents face a multitude of pressures from all angles, including the demand for perfection in a fast-paced, constantly changing environment. They struggle to balance their busy work lives with enjoying important family time, where they are truly present. At the same time, children's levels of activity, confidence, focus and concentration have plummeted, while obesity, bullying and stress have all shot up.

The Warrior Method provides a solution. I know from my own research and experience that martial arts can be a powerful driving force for young people's self-development, and I have discovered that ancient solutions can solve modern problems.

The Warrior Method is my four-step programme for character development. It has transformed the lives of thousands of young people in the UK. I have taken ancient lessons from the dojo (the traditional training room for martial arts) and its moral code, and applied modern teaching methods, psychological research and self-development techniques. This approach can have a massive impact on your child's development. The Warrior Method provides answers to the questions that parents often ask me:

- How can I develop independence in my child?

- As a single parent, how can I create a network to support or mentor my child?

- How can I find a high-quality education for my child that goes beyond the intellectual and physical and focuses on the mind, body and spirit?

- How can I teach my child to seek challenge and adventure while managing their fears and failures?

- How can I protect my child from the negative influences of technology, such as cyberbullying and distraction, and improve their focus and their grades?

The Warrior Method – A solution to modern problems

I began to develop the Warrior Method in 2011. Between then and 2017, more than five thousand students aged between four and seventeen went through the martial arts programme in the Warrior Academy. I designed the programme specifically to develop the character of young people. Through regular testing, the methods have evolved, and countless case studies, testimonials and statistics support the incredible results the programme has achieved.

The learning and framework of the Warrior Method can be applied to any sport, educational programme or club that wants to put character development at the core of its teaching. Because the martial arts are centred on strong values, they are an excellent choice for parents who want to provide a character-developing education for their child.

The Warrior Method is made up of four key steps:

1. Community

2. Inspire

3. Challenge

4. Lead

The method teaches students principles that will enrich their lives and solidify their learning. To get the best results, students must follow all the steps in the above order. No step can be overlooked.

This book explains each of the four pillars that make up the Warrior Method and how I teach them through martial arts. If you're reading this book as a parent, consider the power an excellent martial arts programme can have on your child. If you're a sports coach, an instructor, a leader or a teacher, think about how you could use the Warrior Method framework in your own classes or programmes.

Developing the character of your child or students will have an astonishing effect on their happiness and success. It will also improve your family life, or – if you're working with students – contribute to the success of your organisation. The effect of a well-developed character from a young age becomes clearer in later life, as we will discover in this book. The lessons learnt and the values passed on create a snowball effect of good decisions, a positive mindset and bold aspirations.

In 2017, we sent a survey to more than one thousand parents who have put their children through the Warrior Method programme. The results were staggering:

- 100% of respondents saw an increase in confidence in their child – comparison of their scores before and after the programme showed an average increase in confidence of 26%

- 100% of respondents said they saw a visible improvement in their child's happiness since joining the community

- 100% of respondents said they had much more confidence that their child was less likely to be bullied and that the Warrior Method programme was the reason for this

- 95% of respondents noticed an improvement in their child's grades, which were up by an estimated 23.3%

- 100% of respondents saw an improvement in their child's focus and concentration after taking part in our Warrior Method programme – comparison of their scores before and after the programme showed an average increase in focus and concentration of 16%

The Warrior Method puts forward the belief that martial arts are different from anything else available to parents. It can provide your child with a strong community that inspires and challenges them, giving them a moral compass that they can use to make their own decisions and avoid peer pressure. It will make your child bulletproof to bullying, give them confidence when moving from primary to secondary school, and help them weather the storm of adolescence. It will amplify their ambition, dramatically raise their self-esteem and confidence and give them outstanding leadership skills. All this sets them on the path to success in life.

How it began

Martial arts have been fundamental to my own life. After a near-fatal parachuting accident, surgeons warned that I would never walk again. In this book, I explain in detail how the 'black belt mindset' fostered through studying martial arts and the pursuit of adventure has helped me recover after years in rehabilitation.

As a young boy in a military family, I often had to move schools. Martial arts helped me to make the transition between different schools and taught me how to deal with bullying, and how to resolve conflict. It also showed me the importance of perseverance, courtesy, respect and the power of strong role models.

I wanted to pass on the strong values, education and opportunity that practising martial arts has given me. After three years of training, studying and working abroad, I moved back to England to create the Warrior Academy. In six years, this martial arts organisation has grown to cover forty locations and teaches more than a thousand students a year. I've worked closely with more than a hundred schools in the UK to develop the Warrior Method, a character-development programme that has transformed the lives of thousands of families.

I have helped young, nervous children become British champions with a black belt mindset. My main role now is to develop martial arts instructors into even more powerful mentors for young people in the UK.

How to use this book

The Warrior Method takes you through a journey of discovery of how martial arts can benefit your child. In Part One, we will look at the main problems parents face in the modern world, including nutrition, activity levels, stress and the effects of social media and smartphones. You will discover how martial arts can provide ancient solutions to these modern problems, giving your child more focus, a moral code and higher self-esteem by learning self-defence.

The rest of the book is split into four parts – one for each the four steps of the Warrior Method. Step one of the Warrior Method is 'community'. You will discover the importance and impact of your child's community and how to define a 'black belt community' that will improve your child's behaviour, reduce negative peer pressure, help them move between schools and make them bulletproof to bullying. This section will give you practical advice about turning your home into a peaceful place that reduces stress and helps your child to develop. So much can be achieved when you have a strong, positive community, so this foundation is vital to your child's Warrior journey.

Step two is 'inspire'. Children who lack inspiration in their day-to-day lives often lack a desire to aspire. This limits their mindset and keeps them from thinking 'big'. For your child's ambition to grow, they need to feel inspired regularly. With inspiration from their community and at home, they will constantly seek to develop and challenge themselves and have a desire to succeed. In this section, you will discover why your child's comfort zone is relevant, what the 'optimal performance area' is and what moving into it can do for your child. You will learn how martial arts can give you, your child and your family inspiration that will challenge your current goals and mindset.

Step three is 'challenge'. Now that your warrior is part of a strong community that inspires them to succeed, we can begin to encourage them to seek out challenges. This chapter puts challenge, success and failure in context, helping your child to analyse their performance in a positive way. It also explains the Warrior Academy systems of goal setting and developing daily habits, which are practical ways of helping children increase their confidence and focus. I'll talk about the importance of encouraging adventure to help your child develop. I'll also go deep into 'fear' and learn why we feel it and how to deal with it.

The final part of the four-step Warrior Method talks about leadership and the importance of teaching our young children these skills. Far beyond teaching our children to lead others, these skills encourage your child's independence. They help your child learn about responsibility, how to be reliable, why attention to detail is important and about having pride. Teaching students to lead solidifies their learning and gives them important social, public speaking and presentation skills. This section also gives you practical tips to help develop leadership skills in your child.

The Warrior Method is full of case studies, interviews and personal stories. These give you insight into an alternative way of getting the most out of your child's development. They look in detail at how the Warrior Method has shaped the lives of young people. You also have access to our online learning environment, WarriorNet. This gives you plenty of practical exercises you can do at home with your young warrior to improve their behaviour, set goals and develop their mindset.

I have written this book for parents, educators, teachers, instructors and students interested in developing the character of young people. It gives you a closer look at a proven methodology that can be applied to any course, club or programme. I hope it gives you a deep sense of the power of character development through martial arts and inspires you to seek a martial arts community for your child.

PART ONE

MODERN PROBLEMS AND ANCIENT SOLUTIONS – LESSONS FROM THE DOJO

CHAPTER ONE

Modern Problems

Many of the difficulties parents face when developing their child's character stem from 'modern problems'. The ancient solutions that martial arts provide can help to overcome these problems. Before we can understand how powerful these ancient solutions are, we need to explore how the modern problems affect young people's lives. I believe they influence three areas of a child's character development: concentration, conduct and confidence.

Enter the smartphone

The smartphone is a powerful tool. It unlocks a huge amount of information, access to instant communication and countless apps for us to use.

Before the internet, if we needed to do research or discover new information we'd visit a library, pull out an interesting book and get reading, trying to find the information that would answer our questions. With the advent of the internet and search engines, we could log in to our computers, go online and get our answers within minutes. Now, with smartphones in our pockets and much faster internet speeds, we can find the answer on Google within twenty seconds.

The smartphone has revolutionised how we learn, communicate and go about our daily lives. Because we can communicate and transfer information so quickly, we can learn much faster too. Brilliant! We're all human, though, and we don't always use this powerful technology to benefit people and solve world problems. With social media apps so cleverly designed to give us hits of dopamine through notifications, we can get stuck for hours on tasks that have no benefit other than mild entertainment.

Have you ever been stuck on your Facebook newsfeed for half an hour and realised you don't know why you are there? You're not alone. As humans, we're easily distracted. The powerful smartphone, which can be an incredible force for good, is also a monster that feeds off your time, concentration and emotional energy.

If adults find it so hard to concentrate because of smartphones, it's even harder for children to cope. Young people are now brought up with a smartphone in hand. A survey of 1,500 parents by Opinium found that on average, UK children had a phone by age seven, an iPad by age eight, and a smart phone by age ten.[1]

Many children are struggling to develop high levels of focus. Researchers at the London School of Economics found that banning mobile phones in schools made a difference to students' achievement.[2] Test scores gathered from thousands of sixteen-year-olds between 2,000 and 2012 showed that smartphone bans boosted their achievement by 6%. If a child was previously underperforming, their scores improved by as much as 14%.

Studies have shown that when we get a smartphone notification while doing a task that needs focus, this costs us a great deal of attention. Notifications that interrupt tasks like studying or doing homework have a major effect on our performance. A recent study on the science of distraction found that each time an office worker was distracted by their smartphone, they took around twenty-five minutes to refocus on their task.[3] Most of us find it incredibly difficult to multitask, and notifications take up a large part of our cognitive space (our ability to think).

1   https://inews.co.uk/news/technology/children-first-mobile-phone-aged-seven-browse-internet-five
2   http://cep.lse.ac.uk/pubs/download/dp1350.pdf
3   https://www.nytimes.com/2005/10/16/magazine/meet-the-life-hackers.html

This all suggests that banning smartphones in schools would be a good solution. But smartphones can be excellent learning tools and speed up learning, and technology is now an essential part of students' development. We should embrace the opportunities smartphones provide, but we also need to make sure students use them for their education and aren't distracted by social media, games or messaging their friends.

Improving students' concentration levels and self-discipline are two fundamental aspects of the Warrior Method. By teaching mindfulness and meditation, the structured programme helps to keep students engaged in their education.

Socialising online

The way we communicate is always evolving. Today, we can communicate instantly with a wide network of peers on social media, so we do a lot of our socialising online. According to a 2012 study by Badoo, 36% of those living in the UK spend more time socialising online compared to face to face.[4] The average online Brit spends 4.6 hours a week talking to friends online and only six hours a week talking to people in person, according to Yazino, the online gaming company.

---

4   www.marketwired.com/press-release/generation-lonely-39-percent-
    americans-spend-more-time-socializing-online-than-face-1648444.htm

With almost two billion users a month at the time of writing, the largest social media network is Facebook. Its CEO Mark Zuckerberg recently revealed a new mission statement: to 'give people the power to build community and bring the world closer together.'

Instant communication, the ability to share ideas and information, a wide support network of friends and the ability to stay in touch with people who live far away are all great benefits of social media. Young people are more connected, can express themselves freely and can link up with like-minded peers. They can keep up to date with distant friends they might otherwise have lost touch with.

Online socialising has had a profound effect on how people interact. For example, we can choose to display our lives in a beautiful way that doesn't always reflect the reality. There is now far more desire to share with people we barely know the things we are doing. In many ways, we're more concerned about showing we're having fun online than having fun in real life. All this damages a person's self-worth, self-esteem and confidence. It affects their values and the decisions they make. It influences the development of their social skills, body language and ability to build rapport.

Cyberbullying is a huge downside of socialising online. It's far easier to bully others on social media than it is in person, and the results can be devastating.

Students with disabilities are often a target, and this is carried on in their face-to-face interaction.

The important communication skills learnt through regular practice in person are not developed as effectively online. The virtual world is full of outspoken young people who are more reserved in face-to-face interactions. This lack of development has a strong effect on everything we do: developing friendships, building relationships and even attending interviews.

Socialising online can also lead to revealing too much information about ourselves. It's easier – and feels safer – to give out information online than it is face to face. This can create a whole host of problems and put young people's safety at risk.

Socialising online has the power to damage young people's confidence and self-esteem as they try to keep up with the 'perfect' lives that their friends have portrayed. Added to this, productivity levels plummet because of the distractions caused by social media. This has a huge effect on school work, grades and studying.

We can't – and shouldn't – escape socialising online. It can be a fantastic tool, but we need self-discipline and a strong offline community. Step one of the Warrior Method – community – provides a framework for solving many of these problems.

Activity levels

Levels of physical activity are now lower than ever before. New research suggests that young people's activity levels drop long before they leave school – from the age of seven. The new generation of digitally dependent children are developing inactive lifestyles before they reach adolescence. The Gateshead Millennium Cohort study tracked more than five hundred children for eight years to measure their activity levels. The findings showed a particularly large drop in activity among boys aged between seven and nine. Boys' activity levels dropped from one hour and fifteen minutes of vigorous activity a day at age seven to just fifty-one minutes a day by age fifteen.[5] Girls' activity levels were shown to drop from sixty-three minutes a day at age seven to just forty-one minutes a day by age fifteen.

The study showed that a big influence on children's activity levels was the time they spent on smartphones and computers. Another factor was that they were driven to school instead of walking. It's clear that one of the silent killers in the UK is inactivity. Even before students leave school, this silent killer is setting them up for a sedentary lifestyle. It's important to have funding for sport in schools, but grants for equipment aren't enough. We need to see using our bodies and

---

5   https://telegraph.co.uk/news/2017/03/14/children-become-less-active-age-just-seven-major-study-finds

being active as a normal part of our routine, and build physical activity into our daily habits.

The effects of a sedentary modern lifestyle are devastating. They include obesity, cardiovascular problems, weaker immune systems, and weaker bones, joints and organs. New studies have started to look at how a sedentary lifestyle can increase anxiety, an effect that is often overlooked.

PHYSICAL INACTIVITY

HEART
Your heart muscles grow weak and it becomes a strain to do basic activities

SKIN
Lack of nutrients leads to unhealty skin and hair, exhaustion, headaches, low moods and difficulties in concentrating

STOMACH AND INTESTINE
Can cause constipation

LUNGS
Produce less oxygen

OTHER ORGANS
Your body becomes weak and more likely to become sick

MUSCLES AND JOINTS
When you do not use your muscles, you lose muscle mass, gain weight more easily and become weaker

BONES
Can weaken bones and cause osteoporosis

Anxiety levels

There has been a rapid increase in anxiety disorders in recent years. Although many different things increase anxiety (including social media, a growing population and air pollution), there is a clear link to a sedentary lifestyle. A study from the Anxiety and Depression Association of America showed that among forty million adults, 18% suffered from anxiety.[6] High anxiety levels have a strong influence on our mindset, how we view our life and the world around us, the decisions we make in life and, ultimately, our happiness.

When young people have less active lives, it affects their mental health as well as their physical health. Keeping young people involved in an active community that seeks to develop mind, body and spirit is the solution that the Warrior Method offers.

Ninja nutrition

Nutrition has a profound effect on behaviour. A healthy, balanced diet is crucial to young people's growth and the development of their minds. A side effect of our fast-paced modern lifestyles is that children are often given unhealthy food to eat. It's now clear that as well as the damaging effect this has on

---

6   https://adaa.org/about-adaa/press-room/facts-statistics

health, it contributes to behavioural problems – for example, attention deficit disorder (ADD), attention deficit hyperactivity disorder (ADHD), irritability and aggression.

Young people with ADHD may have one or more of the following symptoms:

- Difficulty concentrating and less focus
- Easily distracted
- Easily bored
- Difficulty organising or completing tasks
- Prone to losing things
- Difficulty in listening
- Difficulty in following instructions
- Fidgety behaviour, squirming
- Extreme difficulty being still and quiet
- Impatience

As young people develop into adults, they may develop one or more of the following symptoms of ADHD:

- Difficulty focusing and concentrating on a task, project or conversation

- Overwhelming restlessness (emotional and physical)
- Frequent mood swings
- Prone to anger and a hot temper
- Disorganised
- Low tolerance of people, situations and surroundings
- Unstable relationships
- More likely to suffer from addiction

The exact cause of ADHD is unknown. Having said that, research has linked an increase in sugar intake over a long time to several symptoms associated with ADHD. It's generally understood that ADHD is related to chemicals in the brain being disrupted, which can affect parts of the brain that are linked to our reward systems.

David Schab, a psychiatrist at Columbia University Medical Center, carried out a full meta-analysis – that is, a study of all the studies – to try to get to the bottom of the connections between certain additives and symptoms.[7] Schab explains, 'Our study showed that the average effect on children's behavior was distinctly larger than the more widely recognized effect of typical lead exposures on children's cognition...

---

7   https://experiencelife.com/article/connecting-adhd-and-nutrition

Untold billions of dollars have been spent to remove lead from gasoline and paint, but hardly any outcry, attention or resources have been mobilized to remove artificial dyes from the food supply.'

In the aftermath of Schab's report came a landmark study from the University of Southampton in the UK. The study involved just under three hundred children. Strikingly, the results showed that food additives could even make children without ADHD hyperactive. The children who did have ADHD became even more hyperactive.

Today, ADHD is usually treated with medication, such as Ritalin and Adderall. These have both been linked to suicidal thoughts and personality changes. Holistic solutions do exist – for example, an 'elimination diet' that provides the nutrition needed for development without introducing harmful additives or colourings that have been linked to ADHD.

Another solution to this modern problem is to train the mind to help children manage the symptoms. Studies have shown that teaching mindfulness and meditation has a strong effect on children with ADHD, and these tools are two of the cornerstones of the Warrior Method.

Let's wrap it up

In this chapter we have discussed the unique challenges that have developed from the modern lifestyle. These modern problems include a decrease in concentration caused by smart phone usage, an increase in anxiety prompted by the idealised images circulating on social media, and the rise of cyber bullying. These have been complemented by a sharp decrease in activity levels, prompting health concerns, and a deeper understanding of the correlation between a modern diet and behavioural problems. Our proposed ancient solutions from the dojo target these problems by:

- Developing a strong inner voice
- Building a child's self-esteem and perception of self-worth
- Focusing on calming the mind through meditation and mindfulness training
- Forming a supportive community with a strong moral code and a focus on living an active lifestyle as a priority and a daily habit

CHAPTER TWO

Parents' Problems

Stress levels are up

Stress is part of being human, and it's not always a bad thing. It's simply how our body responds to the taxing demands placed on us by changes in our environment. There's a difference between 'eustress' (which means positive stress) and 'distress' (negative stress).

Eustress can be motivating and focus your energy. It lasts for only a short time. It can be exciting and improve your performance. A few examples of things that may cause eustress are:

- Getting a promotion for work
- Buying a new home

- Competing in a sporting event

- Being presented with an award in public

Distress can cause anxiety. It can last for a long time, weaken your performance and lead to mental and physical problems. A few examples of things that may cause distress are:

- The death of a family member

- Losing contact with friends and family

- Divorce

- An injury or illness

- Bullying

It's often argued that stress levels in parents are higher now than they were forty years ago. This includes negative stress: distress. In the national Stress in America survey, an annual analysis by Harris Interactive for the American Psychological Association, 35% of adults polled since 2007 reported feeling more stress this year compared with last year, and 53% said they received little or no support from their health care providers in coping with that heightened stress.[8] Stress is a perception that is translated into a physical response. In other words, our mind's interpretation of stress becomes the reality that we feel.

---

8   http://healthland.time.com/2013/02/07/the-most-stressed-out-generation-young-adults

The stresses of modern life include:

- Higher work demands on both parents
- An older retirement age
- A higher rate of separation and single parenting
- Less holiday time
- A less active lifestyle and the problems linked to this (listed in chapter 1)
- A worse diet and poorer nutrition
- A lack of connection to each other, in many cases because we do more of our socialising online
- An increase in depression and anxiety

It's shocking and sad that teenagers are now reported to be more stressed than adults. A survey by the American Psychological Association in 2014 found that '30% of teens reported feeling sad or depressed because of stress and 31% felt overwhelmed. Another 36% said that stress makes them tired and 23% said they've skipped meals because of it. On average, teens reported their stress level was 5.8 on [a] 10-point scale, compared with 5.1 for adults.'[9]

---

9   https://www.nbcnews.com/health/kids-health/teens-more-stressed-out-adults-survey-shows-n26921

Depression and anxiety, which are linked to stress, begin young in students. There is an epidemic of stressed parents raising stressed children. I believe that stress can be contagious, and several studies support this. Research has shown that babies and young children can manifest the physical symptoms of their mother's stressful experiences. The earliest lessons we learn about how to manage stress and strong negative emotions come from our relationships with our parents in our day-to-day lives.

How stress affects your and your child's health

Here are the most common health problems caused or worsened by stress:

- Cardiovascular disease and hypertension
- Depression
- Anxiety
- Infertility and irregular periods
- Frequent colds
- Insomnia and fatigue
- Trouble concentrating
- Memory loss
- Loss of appetite or too much appetite
- Digestive problems

Stress also affects the body's ability to repair itself. Our bodies are incredible machines that can fight infections, kill cancer cells and even fuse together broken bones. The horrifying reality is that these self-repair systems don't work efficiently when we are stressed.

With stress levels up in parents and children, and stress being passed from parents to child, it's more important than ever to manage and reduce negative stress.

Family life

Family life has changed. As parents, our lives are busier, we have more work commitments and when we are at home we're more distracted than ever by new technology and social media. That all affects the quality of the time we spend with our children – and, I believe, their character development. To be able to solve these problems and enrich our children's lives, we must face up to the uncomfortable truth. Let's look first at how the structure of the family has changed in the last forty years.

Families have become more diverse. Once, couples moved in together after they were married, and soon after this they would have children. Today there are fewer marriages, more divorces and more civil partnerships. These things are challenging the status quo.

In 1971 the average household size was 2.9 people. By 2006 this had dropped by 17% to 2.4 people. According to the Office of National Statistics, the divorce rate has risen from 25% of all marriages in 1973 to 55% of all marriages in 2006.[10]

New statistics from Gingerbread, an organisation supporting single parents, suggest that more than two million families in the UK are run by a single parent.[11] This is 25% of all families with children. It's important to note that separation or being in a single parent family is not something that leads to poor outcomes for children; how a family works is more relevant than how it is made up. That being said, any change in the family structure can create stress for parents and children.

As part of a survey in 2017, the Warrior Academy asked more than one thousand members about what they would change in their lives. 90% said they wished they had more time with their children, and 95% said that not having enough time was the thing that caused them the most stress. Our findings agree with research commissioned by Highland Spring on 10,000 families in the UK. Six in ten parents said they struggled to get the family together as a whole. This is partly because children wanted to get away

---

10 https://www.education.gov.uk/publications/eOrderingDownload/
     Appendix-G_SIRC-report.pdf

11 https://www.gingerbread.org.uk/policy-campaigns/publications-index/
     statistics

from the rest of the family to use phones, computers or other gadgets. It means that fewer families are eating together at the end of the day, a time when parents would engage with their children and pass on their values.

The study also showed that energy levels are lower than ever and that time is at a premium. More than 60% of parents admitted that when they do a family activity together, it is normally something physically inactive, such as the cinema, TV, games or sitting and doing something in silence together. They were often distracted by their phones and few activities were active or took place outdoors, which would benefit all by encouraging a healthy lifestyle. A shocking 25% of all parents admitted that they only spend thirty-four minutes a day with their children without being distracted by the stresses of modern life.

All this shows us that the family unit has changed, it is less stable than it was in the past, and families are spending less quality time with each other. These changes are having an effect on young people. With parents and children spending less time together, there is a breakdown of family bonds and communication. Studies have shown that children who spend less quality time with their parents, and so do not develop such strong bonds with their parents, may engage in higher levels of risky behaviour, aggression and delinquency.[12] On the other hand, parents who have a strong bond with their child are more likely to help them through difficult times and reduce their emotional distress. Parents who spend more time with their children are also more likely to help them with their homework or read to them, which aids their education.

Modern problems in the family, with families spending less time together and being more distracted, are having a strong influence on the development of character in children. Ancient solutions can improve the quality of family time by reducing the power of distractions and improving behaviour, which reduces stress at home and problems in school. Strong mentoring can provide a foundation of values to help young people counter the negative influences of peer pressure and deal with emotional distress.

School problems

I believe parents are struggling to find a personal, holistic education for their children that trains the mind, body and spirit.

Young people spend much of their lives in school. I believe the mentoring that they receive in today's education system is not as personal as it could be,

---

12   https://www.psychologytoday.com/us/basics/adolescence

and this is due to the great pressure on teachers. Our teachers play a big role in shaping the lives of our future generations, but they are taken for granted. Teachers are now more stressed, overworked and underpaid than ever before.

A survey by the *Guardian* in 2016 found that '98% of teachers are under increasing stress and 82% say their workload is unmanageable'. So much so that '43% of state teachers in England plan to leave'. New research has been conducted as part of the biggest inquiry into primary education in England for forty years. The findings suggest that the focus on results and initiatives has created an impersonal educational system.[13] The report also said many older teachers felt they had lost the freedom to run their own lessons in the face of government 'micro-management of their work'.

Outside the curriculum, few after-school activities develop the mind or spirit. For example, many team sports focus on the physical aspect and do not provide an education in self-development.

---

13 This study was conducted by Liz Jones, Andy Pickard and Ian Stronach at Manchester Metropolitan University as part of the Cambridge Primary Review. https://www.express.co.uk/news/uk/41698/Impersonal-education-criticised

Let's wrap it up

In this chapter we have discussed parents' problems, and in particular how stress levels are higher now than before for both adults and teens, and the effect of stress on our health and long-term wellbeing.

The changes in the family unit and less time together as a family have an effect on child development, causing children to partake in riskier behaviour and to become more open to the influence of peer pressure. This is exacerbated by the problems we are currently facing in the education system, including an impersonal teacher–student relationship and teachers' unmanageable workloads.

Through martial arts, though, students are taught to calm the mind through meditation, and our studies have shown our programme decreases the stress of parents at home. Being part of a martial arts community also provides young people with a strong moral code in the context of a supportive and positive community. There is a unique bond from instructor to student within martial arts. For thousands of years, students have been mentored through martial arts, demonstrating that there is indeed an ancient solution to modern problems. I believe that the study of martial arts offers a unique perspective on educating young people. As a sport or art for individuals, martial arts gives students the opportunity to work on their own goals while being part of a friendly and safe community. Martial arts classes usually focus on developing strong values and overcoming problems in school or at home, such as bullying, peer pressure, lack of focus and stress.

CHAPTER THREE

Ancient Solutions

My introduction to martial arts

I was introduced to martial arts in 1996, when my father enrolled me in my first tae kwon do club. I was fascinated by, and looked up to, my instructor. As part of a large army family, my three siblings and I moved around a lot. I had recently moved into the area from Aldershot, where I had been failing academically in a school with forty children in each class and a high turnover of teachers. I didn't have a strong male role model at primary school – in fact, there were no male teachers at all. I had a fantastic father who taught me a great deal about life, but he was often away with the army for months at a time.

I developed a mentor–student relationship with my instructor, Michael Tucker. Michael brought out the best in me, teaching me the importance of focus, developing my confidence, honing my competitive spirit and passing on strong leadership skills. He constantly reinforced the strong values and tenets of tae kwon do: courtesy, integrity, indomitable spirit, self-control and perseverance.

Over time, I began studying tae kwon do under Michael every day. I was taken to different places in the UK to compete in national competitions. Winning titles in the English, British and West of England championships had a visible effect on my confidence, which was reflected in better grades in school. The strong community at the club mentored me through changing schools and dealing with bullying. It gave me the strength of character to resist caving in to peer pressure and making bad decisions that would have changed the course of my life.

By age eighteen I had studied tae kwon do for over twelve years and was a second degree black belt. I had also focused on boxing and Thai boxing for several years. I would regularly teach the younger students in the class – an important aspect of any character-development programme is to develop leadership skills.

Martial arts gave me the confidence to tackle challenges head on. At age seventeen I cycled across the Sahara Desert on an old mountain bike, and at eighteen I left home to live abroad. I continued travelling for three years, filling my life with adventure. I made this decision to travel shortly after moving to Denmark to work as a chef and study architecture at university in Aarhus. Starting with India, three years of travelling taught me a huge amount. I studied traditional Muay Thai (also known as Thai boxing) at gruelling camps in Thailand for six months (training for eight hours a day), returning over the next three years for a total of eighteen months. In 2013 I made my professional debut, competing in full-contact Thai boxing. My thirst for adventure and pushing my limits took me on more than five hundred skydives and base jumps around the world. This involved discovering some of the most beautiful landscapes and mountains in the world, and then jumping off them (with a parachute).

I wanted to pass on the valuable lessons I had learned through studying many different martial arts, so I returned to the UK in 2010 to create my own martial arts organisation, the Warrior Academy. To further my knowledge, I studied Brazilian Jiu-Jitsu every day for two years. I also studied Krav Maga, Kung Fu and Wing Chun. Through martial arts I gained the leadership skills to teach other instructors about the Warrior Academy mission and build its impact to more than a thousand students a year.

The origin of martial arts and the moral code

The martial arts have a long and fascinating history. By looking back to where it all began, we can get a clearer picture of why martial arts, as self-development tools, are so effective in solving the modern problems we face.

It's hard to trace the true beginning of martial arts, but evidence shows that it has existed for millennia. The earliest traces were found in patterns in tombs and caves around the world displaying mock combat. Evidence suggests that the classical era (between 10,000 and 6,000 BCE) marks the beginning of tradition in combat and specific martial arts styles – mostly wrestling styles in the form of shuai jiao, Greek wrestling and those described in the Indian epics.

China became the unofficial capital of martial arts when, in 2,000 BC, Emperor Huangdi, who was an expert in shuai jiao and pole-fighting, ensured his troops spent time studying martial arts. Mongolian tribesmen introduced a new style of wrestling to China around 770 BC; this art is believed to be the forefather of sumo wrestling. The Mongolian style of wrestling also entered Korea and Japan, where it developed into individual arts. Records indicate that over generations, the arts spread from China into India and Europe and Asia Minor (the Middle East).

A moral code

Most martial arts teach their practitioners to live by a strong moral code. Let's look at some of the codes of the most popular arts, which have been taught for hundreds of years.

- Judo, from Japan, has a set of eight ethics: courtesy, courage, honesty, honour, modesty, respect, self-control and friendship.

- Many modern arts have their origins in kung fu. The moral code that kung fu masters advocate is known as 'Wude'. Wude is composed of two words: *wu*, meaning martial, and *de*, meaning morality. Wude has two parts: the morality of the mind and the morality of deeds.

- Tae kwon do, from Korea, has the five tenets: courtesy, integrity, indomitable spirit, self-control and perseverance.

- Bushido is the moral code of the samurai in Japan. It has eight virtues: rectitude, courage, benevolence, politeness, sincerity, honour, loyalty and self-control.

Many other ancient arts promote their own set of ethics, morals or tenets. The moral code is a form of character development that is ingrained in the training and tuition. It forms the foundation for learning and is fundamental to the education of the practitioner.

These arts have been passed on from instructor to student, and from generation to generation. They've provided a character-development education to thousands of young people. There is a strong bond between instructor and student, and many arts hold in high regard the disciple-like journey that students take as they develop through each style or art.

Traditionally, these arts were passed on to future generations, who followed in their instructors' footsteps and eventually taught their own students. For many arts, the lineage of instructors is vital to the integrity of the art. For more modern arts, the importance lies in the practitioner's experience, and having training in several arts can build this experience to complete them as a martial artist. An example of this is mixed martial arts, which combines the stand-up striking of Muay Thai and boxing, the grappling and throws of wrestling and judo, and the ground fighting of Brazilian jiu-jitsu to build an all-round martial artist. This is ideal for open style competitions and self-defence.

It's clear that the roots of martial arts are in providing a strong framework and structure of morality to the lives of its practitioners, while empowering the practitioner with the ability to defend themselves.

The mind, body and spirit approach of many martial arts is something I have found parents are unable to source for their children through other available clubs or classes. Many solutions to the modern problems described in chapter 2 are presented in the martial arts. Students are studying an art and its ancient roots, while benefiting from the traditional goals and benefits of an extracurricular club: better health and fitness and an active lifestyle.

The following comments from parents give an insight into their view of the structure, ethos and moral code of the Warrior Academy.

Both of my children enjoy their time at martial arts, which provides them with structure, respect, discipline and the opportunity to develop their maturity and leadership qualities.

Fortunately, both my children are hugely confident. Their martial arts journey has allowed them to exploit that confidence further and channel it by demonstrating to their group, themselves and us as parents (while grading) how much more confident and mature they have become since starting.

Both of them have recognised how they are changing their views on immaturity within school (which is great) and this change has been commented on by their teachers.

I feel that the values and standards of simple discipline and respect that they have further learnt from the Warrior Academy in particular, have complemented both my children in a greater understanding of right and wrong – in my opinion, this is a vital learning experience for any child.

The Warrior Academy continues to instil structure, discipline and rigour to all avid followers. I enjoy watching my children learn self-control and respect and further their journey along the Warrior Academy path. This includes them relishing in the delivery and support to others in their group.

Barry, father of two Warrior Academy students

A holistic solution

While wingsuit base-jumping in Lauterbrunnen, Switzerland, I suffered a terrible parachuting accident. I broke one leg, both ankles and both feet. Martial arts gave me the mindset and determination I needed to walk again, even though surgeons had explained that it would not be possible. After two years of rehabilitation, practising low-impact martial arts like Brazilian jiu-jitsu, I was able to gradually bring my body back to full strength. In fact, I was more flexible and in better shape than ever before – within eighteen months of the accident I was competing in the Brazilian jiu-jitsu British Championships. We'll return to this personal story later in the book.

Practising martial arts has given me the community, mindset, life lessons, values, confidence and leadership skills I needed to fill my life with success and happiness and to overcome adversity. Looking back, it's clear that everything good in my life has stemmed from martial arts. I now work hard to give back to the community that has helped me so much. I do this by developing young people and increasing the awareness of martial arts as a powerful character-development tool.

My story attests to the enormously positive influence that martial arts can have on a person's life, but I'm not alone. Hundreds of parents have shared their feelings with me about the Warrior Academy programme and the effect it has had on their child's development.

I believe the true effect comes later, as we look back and join up the dots. The small seeds that we as mentors plant in the minds of our young students grow into acres of value.

In the first two chapters I described the many problems that modern families face and the effect of these on the development of character in young people. Many of these problems stem from developments in technology, changes in the family unit, busy work lives and socialising online, all of which are hard to change. I believe we can look to martial arts and its ancient framework of mentoring to provide a solution.

Breakthrough areas

In my opinion, resolving three main modern problems has the biggest and quickest impact on a young
person's life. We call these the 'breakthrough areas'.

Concentration. Many students suffer from poor focus,
which affects their grades, ability to apply themselves
and success in life.

Confidence. Many students have low confidence or
self-esteem, which affects their outlook on life and
how they see and react to challenges.

Conduct. Many students have poor behaviour and are
surrounded by a negative community that influences
the decisions they make.

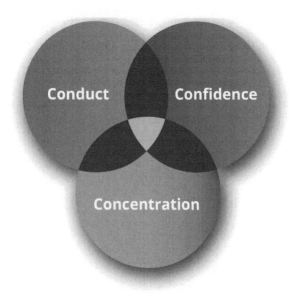

The Warrior Method: A black belt character

The Warrior Method outlined in this book equips each child with three main things:

- Black belt concentration
- Black belt confidence
- Black belt conduct

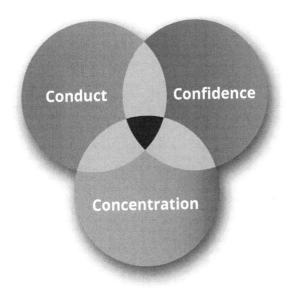

This is the result of breaking through the three main modern problems. To explain each of these, I draw on the statistics and comments gathered from the 2017 Warrior Academy survey of more than one thousand parents who put their children through the programme.

Black belt concentration – to improve focus and grades

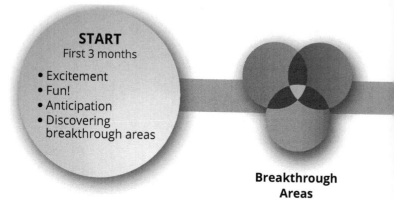

START
First 3 months

- Excitement
- Fun!
- Anticipation
- Discovering breakthrough areas

Breakthrough Areas

In response to our survey:

- 100% of respondents saw an improvement in their child's focus and concentration after taking part in the Warrior Method

- Children's focus and concentration increased by 16% when comparing 'before and after' scores

- 95% of respondents noticed an improvement in their child's grades because of the increased focus their child had developed

- On average, children improved their school grades by 23.3%

Martial arts, and specifically the Warrior Method, have such a strong effect on improving students' levels of

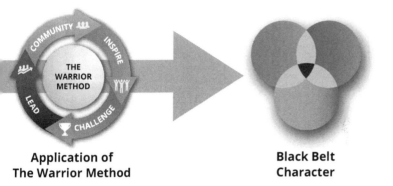

**Application of
The Warrior Method**

**Black Belt
Character**

focus and concentration because they teach mindfulness and meditation. We teach students how to sit and listen to their own thoughts, guiding them through meditation on their first class and encouraging them to prepare for class with a moment of meditation. As we teach our students about stress, anxiety and dealing with a busy life, many of them have learnt to deal with situations preventing them from controlling their emotions. Combining this with homework and an online learning environment has had incredible results.

As part of the Warrior Method programme, following the advice and teaching, my children use their meditation exercises at home and on the school run. The other day my child explained to me that they were really angry and stressed with their siblings

during a game and they took some time out to
meditate or 'practise self-control' as the Warrior
Academy explains and they instantly calmed down
and forgot about what angered them in the first place.

Sam, father of a Warrior Academy student

Dr Lidia Zylowska and her team of researchers at the
University of California found that '78% of participants
who practiced mindful awareness reported reduction
in their ADHD symptoms'.[14] This groundbreaking
study caused quite a stir and – not surprisingly – a rev-
olution in how mindfulness and meditation are used
to assist young people with ADHD. It's an ancient
solution that has been around for centuries, but with
today's distractions and high numbers of children
with ADHD it has never been more relevant.

We put 'sequencing' into our activities, because there
is a strong link between sequencing and concentration. For many children who struggle to concentrate,
following a set order for techniques and exercises
helps them focus. Traditional martial arts are typically very disciplined. We have found that embedding
sequencing (arranging activities in a specific, easy-
to-follow and structured order) into our programme,
exercises and drills, helps students to focus, leading
to a strong correlation with improved concentration.

---

14   https://mindfullyadd.com/adhd-mindfulness-craze

Here's a story about a student of ours:

The Warrior Academy has helped my son in many ways, outside of the martial arts class and even in other clubs. This story is a great example... there is a boy at the badminton club my son attends who frequently gives negative comments, has disruptive behaviour and distracts everyone. One evening it must have been worse than before and my son couldn't focus on the game. He was frustrated with the boy. He decided to take some time out and went to the changing room, out of the way, and he started some meditation that he learnt at the Warrior Academy. After a few minutes he felt better and went back to the game. We felt so proud of him that he could deal with that kind of situation. He has definitely moved on.

Claire, mother of a Warrior Academy student

Black belt confidence – to develop self-esteem and mindset

In response to our survey:

- 100% of respondents saw an increase in confidence, and the average increase before and after the programme was 26%

- 90% said that their child showed less anxiety and was happier after joining the Warrior Academy;

on average, their happiness rose by 8% after
joining the programme

The Warrior Method teaches that challenging our students is vital to their development. We put the word 'challenge' into context, giving young people an understanding of what success and failure are and how they both play an important part in our growth. To get the best results, we also make sure there is always support for each child.

I believe that preventing children from going through challenging times and discouraging them from facing challenges harms their development and chances of future success. From a young age, children must be taught how to overcome obstacles and how to deal with failure and success. Having said that, each child needs to be part of a strong, positive community before challenges can be set. A supportive peer group will provide the help they need to make each challenge a positive learning experience. This helps them learn the importance of perseverance and the development of a black belt mindset.

Martial arts also give students the ability to defend themselves. Although they would rarely need to use this in modern combat, the belief that they can defend themselves and their loved ones gives them a strong sense of confidence. Developing self-esteem through self-defence is unique to martial arts – no other sport provides this for our children.

Black belt conduct – to develop strong values, while improving our community

In response to our survey:

- 93% of respondents saw an improvement in their child's behaviour after joining the Warrior Academy

- This resulted in less stress at home and better quality family time

In martial arts there is a strong emphasis on developing core values of integrity and courtesy. Communicating with each other in a respectful manner is rewarded and encouraged from the start. For example, the way we bow when we enter the room and how we react to victory or defeat help to create black belt conduct.

Most of the problems that stem from poor behaviour can be improved with a change in community and strong mentoring with core values. In chapter 2, we looked at how the increase in socialising online has created room for negative peer pressure, cyberbullying and increased stress and anxiety. By developing each child's community, we ensure that they are part of a goal-orientated, well-rewarded, supportive and happy environment with strong mentoring. This gives them the skills they need to defeat anxiety and stress and makes them feel part of something incredibly special.

Combining this community with strong values and a moral code develops our students' character, giving them black belt conduct.

Let's wrap it up

In this chapter we have introduced martial arts as a holistic solution to the whole development of a young person. We have looked into the breakthrough areas that form the start of the Warrior Method:

- concentration
- confidence
- conduct

We have also examined the profound effect the Warrior Method programme has had on each of these areas, backed up by our 2017 study.

PART TWO

THE WARRIOR METHOD – COMMUNITY

CHAPTER FOUR

An Introduction To Community

What is community?

Developing a black belt community is the first and most important step in the Warrior Method.

> 'I define connection as the energy that exists between people when they feel seen, heard and valued; when they can give and receive without judgement; and when they derive sustenance and strength from the relationship.'
> — Brené Brown
> researcher at the University of Houston

'A community is the mental and spiritual
condition of knowing that the place is shared,
and that the people who share the place define
and limit the possibilities of each other's lives.
It is the knowledge that people have of each
other, their concern for each other, their trust
in each other, the freedom with which they
come and go among themselves.'
— Wendell Berry
US novelist and poet

In the *Oxford Dictionary of English,* the definition of
'community' is a follows: 'a group of people living in
the same place or having a particular characteristic in
common'.

When I talk about community in this book, I mean
the people your child is surrounded by – their family,
friends, relations, neighbours, classmates and, more
importantly than ever, their online community.

Community and development

The community a young person surrounds themselves with affects their social, cognitive (learning),
emotional and physical development.

Social development

Friends and peers have an obvious effect on a child's
social development. It's through their peer groups

that they learn how to interact with other people their own age and how to relate to each other. Through interacting with their peers they learn to develop social and communication skills and how to build rapport. The important interactions in peer groups give young people a sense of self by encouraging them to think about themselves in relation to others in their group. Socialising with peers also teaches young people about appropriate and unacceptable behaviour.

Physical development

A modern problem that has become a major crisis for society is the danger of leading a sedentary lifestyle. A young person's peer group can have a strong influence on promoting health and fitness as part of daily life. Physical activity can involve socialising – from playing games as a young child to enjoying physical fitness or sporting activities leading up to adolescence.

Cognitive development

Your child's experiences with their peers will affect their cognitive development – that is, how they learn and think – in several ways. They will learn to work in groups and understand the importance of teamwork. It is in their peer group that they can find inspiration, share new ideas and interests, nurture their creativity and develop problem-solving skills.

Emotional development

Experiencing different emotions is vital to the development of a young person, and it's in their peer groups that they develop their self-esteem and coping skills. Arguments and disagreements are all part and parcel of understanding and developing the skills to resolve conflicts. Learning how to control strong negative emotions or feelings of frustration comes from interacting with peers.

Analysing your child's community

It's important to analyse the community surrounding your child to find out whether it's a positive one and to remove them from a community that will do harm. A strong community is the springboard from which we raise our aspirations and mindset. It's the basis from which we develop and learn about relationships. A positive community gives us a sense of belonging, a sense of who we are and a connection to others. We feel safe, loved and valued. Without a strong community, we can feel isolated, unworthy and alone.

We've developed a short exercise to help you quickly analyse your child's community and discover if it is a positive or negative influence. You may have a rough idea already, but spending a few minutes writing your thoughts down can give you deeper insight.

EXERCISE

We're going to look at four different communities that are present in your child's life. First, write down each individual group in the four types of community shown below:

School: Friends, classes

Online: Facebook and other social media

Home: Siblings, other family, neighbours

Clubs: Any clubs (after school/extracurricular)

For each of the communities you've listed, answer the following ten statements. For each 'Yes', score 1 point. For each 'No', score 0 points. Then add up the score for each community.

1. My child speaks highly of others in this community.　　　　　　　　　　　Yes/No

2. This community gives my child interesting, creative ideas which they share with me.　　　　　　　Yes/No

3. This community enjoys physical activity together.　　　　　　　Yes/No

4. This community has always been a positive influence.　　　　　　　Yes/No

5. My child has never been bullied in this community.　　　　　　　Yes/No

6. After spending time with this community, my child feels inspired to achieve.　　　　　　　Yes/No

7. My child looks up to other members of this community and talks about them regularly.　　　　　　　Yes/No

63

8. My child is encouraged to help out at
    this community and lead others.   Yes/No

9. This community always encourages
    my child to achieve more.   Yes/No

10. My child is regularly rewarded for
    success in this community.   Yes/No

Multiply the score you have for each community
by 10. This percentage is the score for each of your
child's communities. A powerful, supportive and
positive community will score between 70 and 100%.
A poor community will score between 50 and 70%.
I'd suggest reducing the amount of time your child
spends in this community or removing them from
it entirely. A community score of under 50% is likely
to be doing harm, so you should remove your child
from it quickly.

The score you have given each community is sub-
jective and it can only provide a rough guide, but
I have found it helpful when first analysing a community, and it can help you to compare your child's
communities.

The power of a negative community

We know the importance of community in a young
person's life from looking at the ways in which a person develops through their community. I believe that
being in a negative community from a young age has a

strong effect on the future of a young person. Let's look at the issues that arise from a negative community.

Bullying. A young person in a negative community is more likely to be bullied and to learn that bullying is the norm. This results in emotional distress or the young person becoming a bully themselves and passing on this learned behaviour. Cyberbullying has also increased with the rise in social media and smartphones. For example, statistics from the National Center for Education Statistics and Bureau of Justice in America show that:

- 28% of American students aged 11 to 18 experienced bullying

- 20% of American students aged 14 to 18 experienced bullying

- Around 30% of young people admit to bullying others in surveys

Lack of aspiration. The lower confidence and self-esteem that come from being in a negative community lead to young people developing a highly critical and negative 'inner voice'. Later in life, this translates into lower aspirations. With no immediate inspiration in their developmental years, young people may see many things as 'out of their reach' and so they may not attempt to achieve more.

Poor conduct. Negative peer pressure can lead to poor decisions or bad behaviour. Eventually, this can result in criminal activity, delinquency and poor attendance in school.

Poor health and fitness. This is likely to get worse in later life and lead to obesity, cardiovascular disease and lower life expectancy.

Less opportunity. Slower cognitive development and lower grades in school translate into fewer opportunities once the young person becomes an adult.

Poorer relationships. Poor emotional development or even emotional distress caused by being in a negative community as a young person can lead to negative relationships later in life.

The power of a positive community

We now know the long-lasting effects that a negative community can have on a young person. Let's look at the four main benefits that a strong, positive community can provide.

Providing emotional support

A positive community helps a young person deal with failure or defeat. Providing a positive perspective teaches the young person to put their ups and downs in life into perspective and ensures they learn the value of perseverance.

The community provides constant support, helping the young person through tough times or transitions. I've seen this make the biggest impact on young people dealing with the loss of loved ones, separation of parents and moving schools. This reduces the harmful effects of these highly stressful situations on a child. It's incredible when you consider how a young person may respond in a negative community, without any support or worse.

A positive community promotes supporting one another and teaching the importance of empathy. This teaching will continue in young people's lives, influencing how they raise their own children. We learn so much from our peers, and empathy is a social skill that adds to our emotional intelligence and certainly improves our character.

In a positive community a young person develops strong relationships with other members and enjoys spending time in the community. This will make them happier.

Encouraging health and fitness

In a positive community, young people take part in a healthy physical routine that promotes a healthy lifestyle. This can prevent obesity, stave off health problems and reduce the chances of anxiety and depression.

The community also encourages healthy eating and understands its importance. This can stay with a young person for life, preventing many of the nutrition-based problems we looked at in chapter 1.

The community prioritises a healthy lifestyle when making group decisions. This will ensure the young person enjoys being active and thinks of being active and healthy as part of normal daily life.

Providing inspiration

By providing inspiration, a positive community will increase a young person's aspirations, encouraging them to strive to be the best they can be. This will change how young people see themselves and what they aspire to become. It develops their problem-solving skills, their mindset and, more immediately, their confidence and feelings of self-worth.

A positive community gives a young person perspective on life, encouraging them to see the 'big picture' and giving a deeper meaning to life's challenges and successes. This perspective will also encourage the young person to seek out bigger problems to solve so they can have more impact and become a leader in their community.

Encouraging challenge and adventure

A positive community will build independence in the young person as they seek out challenges and make their own important decisions. This is a skill that will dramatically increase their ability to deal with peer pressure. Peer pressure is less likely to influence them in a negative way as they become accustomed to making their own bold decisions.

It will increase a young person's resilience in stressful situations, give them the ability to lead and inspire others and empower them in their own lives.

A positive community will improve resourcefulness. When tackling challenges in the community, a young person has to think on their feet and they can go on to use this process to deal with other challenges that life throws at them. The old adage 'It's never a lack of resources but a lack of resourcefulness' certainly rings true.

Through the processes of setting and achieving goals, a positive community can greatly increase a young person's confidence and self-esteem. It enriches the young person's life with more opportunities to explore, developing a thirst that will encourage them to learn more about the world they live in. And by promoting healthy competition, members of a supportive community aim to build each other up.

When all four areas are covered and the points listed are achieved, your child will be part of a community that has the power to reshape their life. It will fill them with pride and confidence and give them lessons that will stay with them for life. They'll have a support network that will help them weather the storm of adolescence, prevent bullying and deal with moving schools or the loss of loved ones.

Let's wrap it up

In this chapter we have defined the separate communities a young person may be a part of. We have discussed the influence a community has on a child's cognitive, social, emotional and physical development. We then discussed the power of a negative community, and the effect it can have on children. We also looked at the power of a positive community and how it can be harnessed to reshape their lives.

CHAPTER FIVE

A Black Belt Community

A martial arts community

In the previous chapter I discussed the power of a strong community, and how it can be an incredibly positive driving force. I also talked about the importance of analysing your child's current communities and how you can quickly discover if each one is a positive or negative environment.

Over the years I've been part of many different and exciting communities, including different schools, the military, tight-knit extreme sports communities and martial arts communities around the world. My beliefs were formed from my experience of twenty years in various martial arts communities and in the Warrior Academy. I believe a martial arts community is an excellent example of a positive community in action. In this chapter, I'll explain how this is achieved through the framework provided by many martial arts clubs and in my own organisation. In the face of increasing fragmentation of 'real' (as opposed to virtual) communities, it is more important than ever for children to be able to reconnect with the 'ancient' source of support that is a mixed community of children and adults, teachers and learners, parents and pupils.

Looking at each of the four areas of a positive community outlined in the previous chapter, I'll discuss how, through the Warrior Academy, we develop a 'black belt community'. I'll also explore other ways a martial arts community can benefit your child, including becoming bulletproof to bullying, moving schools, dealing with adolescence and improving life at home – 'the home dojo'.

Here's one parent's insight into our community.

Our (tentative) journey into martial arts and the Warrior Academy began in January 2017, fourteen months ago. Our son Laurie was eight and had had little success with clubs. The advert for the Warrior Academy kept popping up on Facebook and the promise of a free month trial meant he could really experience it beyond the usual first week's high and then the slipping of interest by week three, before we committed.

It took a leap of faith to give it a go. Laurie has a diagnosis of autism and attention deficit disorder; he struggles to stay focused for any length of time, is quick to temper and frequently misinterprets social situations, often leading to aggressive and controlling behaviour. But he loved the idea of martial arts and is sociable by nature. Too many of the reviews by parents talking about their children being able to concentrate in class for the first time became hard to ignore. We felt hopeful and brave and signed up.

I spent the first three weeks peering nervously through a gap in the door, waiting for a meltdown, to be called in, to see Laurie lose interest and wander off. I wasn't alone. When you have a child with social or behavioural difficulties you quickly recognise other children's quirks and their anxious parents waiting in the wings. Yet there was a feeling of disbelief and hope behind those doors. Our sons (in this case) were engaging and playing by the rules, happy and not standing out. They weren't treated any differently. This was a level playing field.

The classes were organised brilliantly and thoughtfully. The less experienced always stand behind the more experienced so they can follow the routines without having to mirror the teacher (which can be hard for anyone with coordination difficulties). The balance of high energy with quiet sitting time; the maintaining of interest with a succession of different exercises and games; the importance of working collectively, so if one person is hurt the whole class stops and has a chance to calm down.

But mostly, the calm and respectful voice of the instructors.

Never a question that each child, whatever their difference, could achieve and do well with the right attitude. No excuses.

As we know, children learn most through example, not what they are told. It wasn't long before Laurie was keen to show me some of the combinations he had learnt, but he wasn't just showing me, he was teaching me, calmly, patiently and respectfully, not showing the usual frustration we were used to.

There have been many highlights in the last year. In Laurie's second week I came to watch the others in the class being graded. In the three- or four-minute sitting session he looked unbearably uncomfortable, swivelling around, opening his eyes. Three months later I was seeing a different child. He could sit still with his eyes closed (mostly) for four minutes (and more recently for five). He was able to coordinate his body and show strength and commitment I had rarely seen before.

His first competition was a massive turning point for us. Both my husband and I admitted afterwards we had never felt so nervous. How would Laurie cope with the noise and busyness of a competition? How would he cope with losing or having someone invading his body space while sparring? We needn't have worried. The day was a revelation. The calm, welcoming atmosphere put everyone at ease. The growth in confidence for all the children was obvious. Laurie came home with a trophy, which was great, but I suspect he got as much joy from being part of something and being able to compete with peers and succeeding at something. Something changed for us too. We saw possibility.

Last week Laurie got his green belt. It felt like a really significant milestone. I'm not sure any of us believed he would stick at something for so long or with such enthusiasm. He goes to three classes a week, travelling an hour each way for one session after a day at school, but it's never a struggle to get him in the car and he's always in a better mood when he comes out. For him the changes have been numerous. Better concentration, improved coordination, gain in strength and fitness and, most significantly, pride in himself. He has a real belief that he can do something as well as other boys his age. For us the obvious pleasure has been watching him stick at something, develop and grow, but also being part of the Warrior community. To watch other people have faith in your child is a powerful experience. It has certainly had an impact on the internal goals I set for Laurie.

Anything is possible!

Victoria, mother of a Warrior Academy student

Emotional support

When a new member joins the club, we have a friendly interview with their parents to find out why their child wants to join, their goals, specific areas to work on, their confidence levels, their behaviour, their fitness levels and so on.

On the first class, the instructor is prepared and ready to welcome the new member to the exciting new community. We give the new member a mentor, someone who is roughly the same age, to help them through the first few classes and make them feel welcomed and supported. After the first class, we discuss with parents how the introduction went. We have another discussion a few weeks later, after the child has achieved certain goals in class and at home. Not only is this good professional practice for any organisation, but it also solidifies the importance of a strong community that provides emotional support.

In the context of martial arts, we refer to each other as 'Sir' or 'Ma'am', a term of respect. This is because the value of courtesy is a vital part of the Warrior Academy programme and traditional martial arts around the world. For a four-year-old, to be called 'Sir' is completely unexpected. The conversation between teacher and student, and between students, is immediately courteous and respectful with this introduction, and this has a profound effect. This approach to communication changes students' mindsets and the decisions they make about their behaviour.

It's vital to foster and build strong relationships with parents so that as children go through hard times or tough transitions outside school, our community can be the constant, positive support that helps them through it all. This is far more achievable with excellent communication between parents and teachers.

As students progress and become more experienced, they are encouraged to lead and help others in the group. This journey from beginner to experienced to leader helps develop the support our new, inexperienced students need. It also teaches students important leadership skills, instils pride and many other traits discussed in the chapter 11 on leadership.

Students learn to achieve individual goals while working as a group to support each other. This aspect is interesting, because it develops teamwork while learning an individual sport. We teach students how to deal with failure with a positive mindset, and how to take a humble attitude to success. Each exercise a child takes part in starts and finishes with a bow and a handshake, reinforcing the importance of respect and courtesy and practising good sportsmanship. In turn, this ensures the community is highly supportive of one another.

Positive action

The value of health and fitness

From the first class, we ensure we pass on the values of health and fitness in a fun and enjoyable way to elicit a positive mindset and attitude around being active and healthy. In every class, we push the students physically by raising their heart rates and keeping them active. At the same time, we follow a conditioning programme that improves their strength gradually. Flexibility is a big part of martial arts, and this increases as students learn more complicated kicks.

What's brilliant about a typical martial arts curriculum is the progressive physical challenges. Students need to do more reps for each bodyweight exercise as they progress through the belts, and their flexibility increases too. The clear progression and structure of the belts promotes an improvement in physicality, strength, flexibility and cardiovascular levels for students in a way that other sports find hard to achieve.

Holding 'mat chats' or 'inspiration talks' should be a focus for all character-development programmes. In the Warrior Method, we take great care to spend time each session teaching strong lessons on important topics, such as nutrition and keeping active, and passing on the many other values that make up the black belt character. These talks last from one to ten minutes, depending on the age group, the maturity level of the class and the relevance of the subject.

Encouraging aspiration

The belt system used in most martial arts is truly inspiring for students. Having clear, tangible goals is vital. It's also important to give new students an opportunity to see advanced students in action. Reinforcing the success of advanced students encourages other students to achieve it themselves. We set personal goals for each student in line with their specific needs, working closely with parents.

We want our students to experience lots of little wins to create a snowball effect of achievement that rapidly builds confidence. To do this, we set small achievable goals and break them down into daily, weekly and monthly targets. Students then begin to feel inspired by what they can achieve. If a child is part of a community where they rarely achieve – perhaps in school or in other clubs – these small wins have an even more tremendous effect on their mindset.

Offering challenge and adventure

On top of the small daily, weekly, monthly and longer term goals, we make sure that students have opportunities to compete and experience adventure. This opens their eyes to what they can achieve and gives them a chance to explore, to build their resilience and to find a sense of adventure. We go into more detail on this in part four, where we explore the power of challenging themselves on a young person's mindset and future life.

Our motto is 'courage earns confidence': by having courage, students will become a better version of themselves. This goes a long way to explaining the benefit of improved confidence.

Making your child bulletproof to bullying

One of the main concerns when a child is surrounded by a negative community is bullying – it can be devastating for students and damage their development. Emotional support is one of a positive community's biggest strengths, and the self-worth this develops in each young person prevents bullying and gives students and parents the peace of mind that it will not happen.

One of the goals of the Warrior Method is to make each child bulletproof to bullying. We use the term 'bulletproof to bullying' to explain one of the greatest benefits the Warrior Method of character development provides. A strong character deters bullies, who often prey on the weak or the easily intimidated. If that strong character is given a moral compass, they become an advocate for preventing bullying and try to stop bullying from happening around them.

In our 2017 Warrior Academy survey, we asked parents whether they had greater peace of mind about bullying. All the parents who responded said they had far greater peace of mind that their child was less likely to be bullied, and that the Warrior Method was responsible. One parent explained, 'Definitely. Not because of the physical aspects of what she's learning at the Warrior Academy but more because of the confidence she gets from a feeling of self-worth.'

We then asked parents if their child was happier because of this. One hundred% of parents agreed that their child was happier now that they had learnt how to deal with conflict, stop bullying and develop self-worth, recognising that we are all different and that this is one of our greatest strengths. Parents explained:

> 'She seems more at peace when talking about others at school, recognising that she is different but more relaxed about it.'

> 'He is definitely happier because the school were always on at him telling him there's something wrong with him and now he is happy just the way he is and is not bothered by what people say.'

I mentioned earlier that being part of a strong martial arts community helped me through many things in my life. Bullying was one of the things that martial arts helped me to overcome. I hope that sharing my personal stories will give you a deeper insight into the power of a martial arts community and how it has shaped the Warrior Method.

Between the ages of seven and ten, I was bullied terribly in school. This came from changing schools and being the 'new kid' in a small class where a tight-knit community had already been established. I was nervous about changing schools, and in this position I was an easy target. I was targeted before school, during break time and after school. I sat alone during lunch. I was bullied physically, at times being held while others took their turns kicking me. Worse by far, though, was the psychological bullying, which was cleverly hidden from teachers and parents. My confidence was shattered. I lived in a rural town with few neighbours or friends, and there was little to look forward to each day when I went to school.

My only solace was my martial arts club. I was part of a community where each child called each other Sir or Ma'am, where courtesy and respect were held as high values and developing a positive mindset was the norm. A tremendous amount of power came from the support I received from this community. I was able to speak freely about what I was going through, see the same friendly faces each day and have one-to-one mentoring with an excellent instructor, who gave me the strength of character I needed to eventually overcome bullying.

Towards the end of this three-year ordeal, my confidence had grown thanks to being part of such a strong community. With a strong sense of self-worth and a newly developed moral compass, I simply couldn't stand the injustice any longer, and I developed the courage to stand up to the main aggressors. It took a tremendous amount of courage to hold my ground, and this resulted in a physical confrontation. That was something that martial arts had given me the confidence to use effectively, and immediately it caused a shift in the pecking order in school.

From a young age, martial arts had taught me that I could overcome bullying by having a strong self-image and a good attitude. Martial arts provided a framework I could use to recover from terrible bullying, both physically and emotionally. Fortunately, thanks to the mentoring I received and the community I was surrounded by, my experiences of bullying shaped me into a confident young man. Without this support network and mentoring, it's likely that I would have become more of a victim, far less confident and happy, and set up to have less opportunity in life.

Learning to deal with bullying is vital. It can make or break a child's character and, as parents, I believe we must prepare for this. I tell my students every week that courage earns confidence. Courage is fostered in a strong community that develops mindset and resilience and has a foundation of emotional support. We can emerge from bullying stronger than ever, with a thicker skin, more resilience and a feeling of self-worth, or we can emerge beaten and broken, with our self-esteem destroyed and problems with developing trust. This can go on to affect our future relationships and the decisions we make and can result in an unfulfilled life.

Although there are some excellent campaigns to prevent bullying or stop it from continuing, it's still a widely debated topic that is hard to solve altogether. Bullying is likely to happen to each of us – as adults or as children. It's imperative that we ensure our children are part of a community that not only protects them from being a victim of bullying but also prevents them from becoming a bully.

To deal with instances of bullying and prevent it from happening at all, we need to understand bullying – why it happens and where it comes from. Unfortunately, bullying occurs naturally in all our communities. It's been going on for thousands of years. What's interesting is that bullying is remarkably simple. In almost all cases, bullying is 'dominance behaviour', and this behaviour usually happens because something in the bully's life is missing. Often, a bully is lacking attention at home and they react by lashing out at others to get attention. They may have learnt this behaviour at home, where parents handle conflict poorly, show aggression or are angry.

A study by Stomp Out Bullying showed that bullies don't need a reason to hurt others.[15] When asked, some replied:

- Because it makes me feel stronger, smarter or better than the person I'm bullying
- Because I'm bullied at home
- Because it's what you do if you want to hang out with the right crowd
- Because I see others doing it
- Because I'm jealous of the other person
- Because it's one of the best ways to keep others from bullying me

Look closely at the reasons why a bully would have behaved as they did. Most of the problems stem from a negative peer group or lack of confidence.

Our two-step method for dealing with the bully

If we notice that a child is bullying others, we follow this approach:

1. First, we discover what's missing and fill in the gaps, replacing the negative with positive and reinforcing that regularly. This changes the

---

15   http://stompoutbullying.org

learned behaviour the bully has built up from being part of a negative community.

2. Then we surround the bully in a positive community where they feel welcome, at home and free to be creative and happy… without fear of being bullied themselves. We know bullying often stems from fear, so eliminating this fear goes a long way to prevent bullying.

We have spotted bullies in the past and transformed them into the biggest advocates for anti-bullying as they begin to learn about the effects of their actions. Instead of harming others, they begin using their evident power of influence for good, gearing it towards building up their friends.

Our six Ps – Six practical steps to overcome bullying

I think looking back the bullying I received at school is one of reasons I have been teaching martial arts full time for the last 10 years. As a martial arts instructor, I've focused on developing the confidence of young people. I began to realise the devastation bullying can have on a child's life and, indeed, how many students actually go through bullying. I began to see young minds completely change and their opportunity and happiness simple fly away due to a negative community.

I began to mentor hundreds of young students through bullying as their martial arts instructor. I also began to see the effect overcoming bullying can have. As in any negative situation or hardship, when we fight back and discover our own courage, we grow. Courage earns confidence.

Over the years I developed a system to help mentor students through bullying. While I've not shared this with a wider audience, I have used it to help countless students in our clubs over the years. These six practical steps can make a massive impact on your child's life.

- Step One: Perception – a shift in our understanding

- Step Two: Presentation – body language

- Step Three: Preparation – preparing to respond

- Step Four: Practice – role-playing games

- Step Five: Produce – an incident log

- Step Six: Persevere – achieve in a separate community

Step one: Perception – a shift in our understanding. So many students don't report getting bullied and it's often because they blame themselves. We need to bring up the subject of bullying by making it clear that no one deserves to be bullied, no matter how flawed or imperfect they may feel.

Educate children on why bullies bully. It's almost always because it makes them feel good because they are missing something. Bullying shows weakness of character, not strength.

Changing the perception of the bully from a threat to someone we should be feeling sorry for reduces the fear of being bullied and prevents us from reacting with aggression or distress. If we respond in this way, a bully has gained the reaction they are after.

Reframing bullying will help your child open up about their experiences and encourage them to participate in the next 5 Ps.

Step Two: Presentation – body language. Body language is everything – a bully is far less likely to target someone who appears strong or confident. So we must teach our students that the way they walk, talk, or even hold eye contact is vital to appear confident.

That's one of the reasons we place such a huge emphasis on developing confidence as part of our programme: we develop the way our students walk, talk, hold themselves, even how they shake hands. What we are teaching them is also vital for developing their leadership skills.

It's amazing to watch this teaching take effect: after a period of time practising being confident, confidence really does become a natural part of the students' personalities.

And because of this new found confidence, they no longer appear to be an easy target.

Step Three: Preparation – preparing to respond. When a child is faced with a bully they will be in an emotional state and unable to form a well-thought-through response. In the worst-case scenario they will go into panic mode, fight or flight will kick in, and they are likely to become more of a victim. But just as we practice martial arts drills and self-defence techniques so that deploying these skills becomes the natural response at a time of heightened emotion, without any conscious thought, we can prepare a child for bullying in the same way.

Work with your child to brainstorm quick and easy come-backs that will make your child appear confident when they are being bullied: simple, non-aggressive phrases like 'go away', 'stop', 'who cares?', 'watch it!', 'whatever'.

Step Four: Practice – role-playing games. As a parent it's highly unlikely that you will be there with them to help when they are being bullied, so a big part of mentoring a child to overcome bullying lies in practice. Role-playing games with your children are a great way to arm them to deal with a difficult situation. These little games can help you in two brilliant ways:

- Often a child may find it hard to articulate what they are going through: they may be shy or find it hard to describe. If you take on the role of the victim and they take on the role of the bully, you will get a great insight into what is actually happening and a deeper sense of the situation.

- You will also get a chance to teach your child the best way to react to the bullying, as described in Step Three.

Step Five: Produce – an incident log. At some point you may find the situation has gone on for too long and your child cannot overcome the situation without help. Teach your child the Five Ws of reporting bullying: Who, What, When, Where and Witnesses. Unfortunately, it's often the bully's word against the victim's – as crazy as this sounds it's important to have a written log of incidents with witnesses, and a little notepad can really help.

Step Six: Persevere – achieve in a separate community. Find something for your child outside of the community they are currently being bullied in, to support them and fill them with confidence, because when we get good at something and we progress, our confidence and self-esteem grows.

As I grew through martial arts as a child, going from belt to belt, growing in confidence, winning competitions and teaching other students, the power of the bullies' words weakened. I began to listen to my own thoughts, and to my own opinions of myself more than anyone else's.

The beauty of martial arts as a tool for overcoming bullying is the focus on confidence, developing a strong mind, handling confrontation effectively and keeping calm in stressful situations.

Using this system, which has been developed over time, has been fundamental to mentoring young students emerge from bullying stronger, more confident and with buckets of courage. I really hope, if your child is suffering from bullying, that you find value in the 6 Ps. If you do, I'd love to hear from you!

Developing understanding

An open community. We hold regular talks with our students, where we encourage them to share their experiences of bullying. This is only possible in a friendly and supportive community, and it does a few important things. When someone is brave enough to share their experiences, they subconsciously give others in the group the courage to share their experiences as well. Sharing makes students more aware of why bullying occurs, how it happens and how to spot it so they can prevent it. They develop a lot of strength from the support they find in our communities, specifically from our chats about bullying.

Understanding individuality. We make a point of teaching our students that their uniqueness is a strength. By understanding that our little quirks, the things we like and don't like, make up our personality and make us who we are, we develop a stronger inner voice. We teach our students to respect each other's individuality in the same way that they should respect their own.

Understanding bullies. We also teach our students to try to understand bullying. Using the information I set out earlier in this section, we talk to our students about how a bully may be going through something similar themselves. This understanding of bullies gives our students a chance to forgive those who have bullied them.

Here's a story about a child who has been through our programme:

It started when my son was in Year 5. He used to come home nearly every day saying that his friends (or I suppose the boys from his year) were annoying him and unkind to him. I wasn't sure whether it was bullying or not. This had been going on for months and just before Christmas when he was in Year 6, I contacted the Warrior Academy. I wanted to give him the tools to stand up for himself, and I was sad and frustrated myself about the situation. I sat down with him and told him that I was going to take him to a new club.

This club would help him to stand up to his friends. I remember I used the words 'it is going to help you fight back' but I explained to him that I don't want him to physically fight with his friends but deal with their behaviours and their negative comments.

At the time, he knew a boy that was going to the club so that reassured him a little. The changes started straight away, he was happy and proud. The following day he told his friends that he was going to go to a martial arts club. I think he felt empowered and maybe reassured that he was not going to feel down any more. And honestly, since that day, I have never heard him say that his friends are bothering him.

He went to his first class and liked it. Now, he has been going for more than two years and does very well. It helps him physically too with balance, flexibility and strength and generally feeling comfortable in his body. He is more confident and happier. As parents, we have been so happy about the changes we've seen. We are pleased that we made the right decision to take him to the Warrior Academy even if I was worried that he was a little old to start martial arts at ten years old, he wasn't at all and always felt very comfortable to go to the lessons.

Claire, mother of Thomas

Moving from primary to secondary school

I've mentioned previously how a strong, positive community can provide the support needed to help us through times of hardship, including, for a young person, difficult transitions. The most common difficult transition young people make is from primary to secondary school from the ages of ten to twelve.

For me, this was a difficult transition. I recall the pressure of developing and entering new social groups, and the higher academic demands were particularly challenging. Having moved between two primary schools before and finding it hard to be welcomed into the new social group, resulting in bullying, I was now faced with a similar problem. I was moving from a small, rural school with less than fifteen people in my year, and none of my friends were making the switch to the secondary school that I was going to. Those joining the new school mostly came from three large primary schools, and social groups had been established for many years. Coupled with this, we had moved to another village and I had not yet formed any social groups or friendship groups there.

The first few months were difficult, as any child would have found. Once again, the martial arts community I was a part of was the only constant in an ever-changing social situation. I saw the same faces every other day and was given the injection of positivity, self-worth and confidence I needed to get me through another difficult transition in my life.

A common mistake I find parents making is to take their child out of any club they've been attending as they go through this transition in the hope they will make new friends and take up new clubs or opportunities in their new school. I believe this to be a mistake for three main reasons:

1. It's a gamble that the child will make friends quickly and not be isolated in their new school. They might not fit in perfectly to one of the new clubs they have an option to join.

2. They might have worked hard to build a strong sense of community in their current club. Taking this away from them at the same time as losing the community of their primary school can be too much of a shock. Consistency and daily or weekly routines (like going to a particular class) can do wonders for maintaining and improving confidence.

3. The benefits of a strong community are built up over many years, so they have a powerful cumulative effect if they child stays in that community. They can teach the new skills they possess to others, and this aspect of leading has a profound effect on their sense of self, their sense of pride and the development of their character.

I believe so strongly that this is a crucial time for students, that each summer we provide scholarships for twenty-five students whose parents are concerned about the move from primary to secondary school. The scholarship is for a free four-month programme, where we focus on developing children's confidence and mindset to prepare them for the new school year.

Weathering the storm of adolescence

There's a biological transition that shakes the emotional foundation of almost every young person as they develop. This is also a time that parents often dread, as their brilliant children can become argumentative, irrational, aggressive, hyper-sensitive, depressed and difficult to live with. Puberty strikes, hormones erupt like a volcano, girlfriends or boyfriends arrive on the scene (with all the emotions they bring) and all rationality goes out of the window.

Usually, adolescence begins between the ages of thirteen and nineteen. It's the time when a child turns into an adult. The physical and psychological changes often begin earlier, though, during the preteen or 'tween' years (ages nine to twelve). Adolescence is no different from other transitions in a young person's life. It's a period when their environment is unsettled – this time, caused by a dramatic change in hormones.

The journal *Psychology Today* characterises it thus:

'…This transitional period can bring up issues of independence and self-identity; many adolescents and their peers face tough choices regarding schoolwork, sexuality, drugs, alcohol, and social life. Peer groups, romantic interests, and appearance tend to naturally increase in importance for some time during a teen's journey towards adulthood.'[16]

The adolescent period is a time when our environment is unsettled. I believe that high emotional intelligence (high emotional IQ), a developed sense of empathy, and a strong sense of self and self-worth all have an excellent, stabilising effect on controlling the strong emotions of adolescence.

The Warrior Method aims to develop students' emotional IQ by encouraging them to think about the effects of their actions and maintaining a strong sense of courtesy and respect. By prioritising strong values as a means to control our own behaviour, we increase emotional IQ. A higher emotional IQ will improve empathy. This gives young people better judgement about how to behave or, if they have behaved poorly, helps them analyse their behaviour and its negative effect on other people more quickly. Ultimately, this results in less sulking, less being

16 www.psychologytoday.com/us/basics/adolescence

isolated in the bedroom, more apologies and quickly repaired relationships.

Many of the problems we've noticed at adolescence centre around self-worth. It's at this time, which can last for many years, that young people are trying to find their place and get a real grasp of who they are and what they are worth. With a negative inner critic and poorly developed self-esteem or self-image, this time can be damaging. A supportive community can provide a structured programme that identifies weak areas, helps young people make big steps to improve them, and provides emotional support. All this gives young people the right protective kit to weather the storm of adolescence and come out well developed and ready for adulthood.

I believe that beyond coping with adolescence, there's much benefit to be gained from this time. A young person asks themselves so many meaningful questions during this period, and with the right mentoring and support network this provides a huge opportunity for introspective enlightenment.

The home dojo

We've talked about a young person's community in school, in clubs and in peer groups. It's now time to talk about their home community, or what we like to call the 'home dojo'. In martial arts, the dojo is a place of respect, courtesy, community and self-development. We refer to our students' homes as the 'home dojo' because we want our students to understand that the lessons learnt in the dojo should be taken home. It's applying these lessons at home that makes the biggest impact.

In part one we touched on the many different elements in parents' lives that increase stress. We discovered that there are more distractions, a higher workload and less time to spend with children than in the past.

In our 2017 survey, we asked parents about the effect the Warrior Method had on them, their children and the whole family. All parents who responded said they saw a marked increase in their child's happiness after joining the Warrior Method programme. 90% of parents said that their stress levels at home had dramatically reduced because their child was behaving better, their child was happier and they had more peace of mind that their child wasn't as likely to be bullied and was more confident. In a separate survey through the Warrior Academy in 2017, 80% of parents said that their child's happiness was the biggest stress factor of their lives, their highest priority and the thing that was on their mind the most.

With 100% of our students becoming happier, we had directly reduced parents' levels of stress. Interestingly, the second most important concern for parents was not having enough time with their children (70% of parents mentioned this). By improving their child's emotional IQ and behaviour, developing their sense of self-worth and making them feel happier, less time at home is spent disciplining or arguing. That means more time is enjoyed in a positive way, improving the relationships between parents and children and between siblings.

What you can do at home

We treat our clubs like families. We plan goals together, treat each other with respect, support each other in difficult times, encourage each other to succeed and celebrate our successes and little wins together. We work as closely with our students as we do with their parents, and we believe some of the exercises we do in class can have an excellent effect at home. Here are a few to try.

Have joint discussions. We hold 'mat chats' in class where we talk about a certain value, encouraging students to take part and get their point across. Leading, putting forward their opinions and thinking creatively goes a long way to improving their confidence in discussions.

Set goals together. We sit down and set goals for the year, the term and the month and, in many cases, the class. By doing this together, the progress we make is measurable and we are all more motivated. Check out chapter 10 for the Warrior Academy goal-setting system.

Encourage daily habits. Creating a small set of daily habits that we do each day can have a profound effect on our mindset for the rest of the day. Check out the section on daily habits in chapter 10 and see if you can do this at home.

Talk openly about challenges. In class we ask students to talk about what they are finding difficult. This helps other students relate, as they may have similar problems. By sharing our problems, we develop a more connected community and a higher level of support. Being open about our strengths and weaknesses is a great way for us all to see our individuality. Try our strengths and weaknesses exercise shown later in this book.

Celebrate success together. As a club we always make a big deal of success. We hold regular award ceremonies in each club after each grading. Parents and friends come together to see their child awarded with their new belt. It's an important part of being a strong community, instilling a feeling of pride and reinforcing the success of our students. By celebrating success at home, you can have a positive influence on your child and their goals.

Let's wrap it up

The foundation of any good organisation or club should be a positive, supportive community. I've explained how the community surrounding a young person affects their social, cognitive, emotional and physical development. Without a strong community, students are less likely to take up challenges.

As the first step of the Warrior Method, we place strong emphasis on developing a black belt community. A black belt community improves behaviour, reduces negative peer pressure, provides emotional support and mentoring, help students move between schools and deal with difficult times, and makes them bulletproof to bullying.

It's now vital that our young people are regularly inspired so that they can live fulfilling and compelling lives.

PART THREE
THE WARRIOR METHOD – INSPIRE

CHAPTER SIX

Inspire

An introduction to inspiration

In this chapter we will be exploring the second step of the Warrior Method: inspiration. I'll explain the significance of sustained inspiration and its power in fulfilling your child's development. You will find out why and how learning martial arts inspires children, and how the Warrior Method is structured to give each student an abundance of inspiration.

Black belt mentoring

'The mediocre teacher tells.
The good teacher explains.
The superior teacher demonstrates.
The great teacher inspires.'
— William Arthur Ward

We can all remember that one teacher who inspired us in school or in a sports club we attended. They brought out a spark in us that encouraged us to be fully engaged, to be creative, to raise our aspirations and to fully enjoy what we were doing. They inspired us to persevere through difficult times, plateaus or roadblocks in our learning. We remember the teacher, more readily than the lessons, because the teacher is the heart of the education system. Without a doubt, an inspirational teacher or leader can be a powerful driving force for a young person's success in life.

In Part One I mentioned that the education system often lacks a personal touch and that it seems more distant now than ever before. Many parents are struggling to find a personal, holistic education that focuses on the mind, body and spirit while catering for their child's individual needs. We've discussed how martial arts tuition focuses on the development of character, which requires the cumulative development of the mind, body and spirit. The relationship between the teacher and the student is also vital to a long-term solution to this modern problem.

I have found that the teacher–student relationship is particularly special in martial arts. In the Warrior Method we call this special bond 'black belt mentoring'. In our clubs, it's created through the style in which our instructors teach, and it's typical among high-level martial arts instructors, senseis and masters.

To become a black belt mentor, a teacher must first practise what they preach and inspire through their own work. Previous experience is fundamental and can be drawn upon for every lesson, from correcting a student's technique to analysing their mindset and redirecting its course onto a positive path. This is a role that is clearly visible in the ancient disciplines of martial arts across the globe. The process of mentoring a student is far more powerful when a mentor can share their own life lessons on how they overcame failure and when they can truly empathise with how students are feeling.

A true martial artist sees martial arts as a lifelong pursuit. There is no end goal. Most new students enter believing that the black belt is the epitome of martial arts success, but this couldn't be further from the case. After the black belt, there is only more learning. There's a crossover between learning martial arts and the pursuit of perfection, and this endless pursuit almost always leads to individuals taking on a teaching role. I'll explain the role of leadership in more detail later. For now, let's understand that in martial arts there is a natural flow from student to teacher, a position earned through experience; from this, we can understand that the all-important personal experience needed to be an excellent mentor is naturally present in martial arts instructors.

'Curiosity dimmed is a future denied'

As a teacher it's important to apply the correct style of teaching. With a large group of young students, a more autocratic style should form the basis of the class to avoid accidents and ensure safety. As students become more advanced or mature, a democratic leadership style can be useful for developing creativity and encouraging individuality. An example of this is peer-to-peer learning.

In the Warrior Method we encourage peer-to-peer learning to draw out this creativity and individuality. Often in class, we put students into small groups and give them tasks to develop a technique, create a combination or discover a solution to a problem. This way of learning gives students inspiration and a sense of achievement, because they have provided their own solution by drawing on their own knowledge and expertise.

Curiosity forms the basis of inspiration. A black belt mentor brings out curiosity in their students. Bruce D. Perry, an internationally recognised authority on brain development and children in crisis, points out,

'Curiosity dimmed is a future denied. Our potential – emotional, social and cognitive – is expressed through the quantity and quality of our experiences. And the less-curious child will make fewer new friends, join fewer social groups, read fewer books… the less-curious child is harder to teach because he is harder to inspire, enthuse, and motivate.'

Martial arts differ from other sports because when a child is studying a martial art, they are studying an ancient art form developed over thousands of years and hundreds of generations around the world. Unlike in many modern sports, where a team or equipment is needed, a martial artist can develop their own skill independently and anywhere in the world, without any equipment. Martial arts open the door to endless learning and excellent forms of self-expression.

It is certainly difficult for a stranger to martial arts to view this perceived 'fighting' as anything like an art. When I first learned Muay Thai, I already had a strong background in western boxing, tae kwon do and kick-boxing. I immersed myself in Thai boxing camps in Thailand, determined to learn what is known as one of the most brutal and effective stand-up fighting arts. Muay Thai is an art that is fought with full contact and uses powerful elbows and knees with devastating effect. To Thai people it's a way of life. They do not overcomplicate their techniques – instead, Muay Thai focuses on a few basic but incredibly effective strikes. When I began studying Muay Thai in 2010, the style felt awkward to me at first because it differed so much from the styles I'd learned: for example, throwing the kick rather than flicking the kick, and using the shin to create a shield to defend yourself against almost all kicks. As I developed from hours of studying a single technique, I gradually built my muscle memory. Over months and years my reaction times shortened and it became second nature.

I went to watch some fights at a stadium in Thailand with my trainer and mentor, Kru Ped. We watched an incredible fight between two experienced Thai fighters. The way they moved, how they reacted to each different strike, their timing, precision and accuracy, and the courage, perseverance and heart of each warrior in the ring, all developed over a lifetime of dedication to an art form, was inspiring. After the fight, the two warriors embraced and raised each other's hand, bowing to each other and each other's trainers. They drank water from their opponent's trainer, as is the tradition. The blood, sweat and tears they put in to execute such perfect technique was truly a display of mind, body and spirit.

My trainer turned to me and said something I'd never forget: 'You see, Seb, beautiful Muay Thai.' There's a flow to every style and art – even the most brutal of arts has incredible history, culture, creativity, accuracy, spirit and beauty. There's a massive amount of inspiration and mastery in each art. Martial arts have the power to stir the soul of any individual – student and teacher alike.

Black belt mindset

We've touched on the importance of an excellent mentor who works with individuals to inspire them and bring out the best in their actions, developing them as a whole person. Each of us has a mentor who analyses our performance and constantly gives us feedback on how we are doing, what we have done right, and what we could improve on. Someone who consoles us in difficult times; someone who gives us the power to step up and conquer challenges, overcome hardship and have the discipline to persevere with a routine. This mentor does not come in the form of a martial arts instructor, our parents or a school teacher. It's our inner critic – the voice inside our heads. Essentially, it's 'us'. When no one else is around, self-talk is a powerful positive or negative force in our life. For many, unfortunately, this can be a negative voice. That negative voice can drown out any positivity and kill inspiration and drive. If your child doesn't have a well-trained inner voice, who is training your child when no one else is around?

I've always been fascinated and inspired by survival stories, from Ernest Shackleton's survival over 105 days in the Antarctic, to the stories of the Chilean miners who were trapped 23,000 feet underground for 69 days after a rockfall. These stories depict the incredible resilience of individuals in devastating and hopeless conditions. In almost every case, their survival was due to a powerful inner voice that refused to give up, that constantly pushed them forward. They displayed true grit and perseverance.

In our Warrior Method we dedicate a significant amount of training time to developing a positive, powerful inner voice. Whether a student stays with us for one month or ten years, we want to teach them things that will stay with them for life. I believe that training the inner voice is one of the most important lessons we can deliver, which is why we place such a significance on it during class.

In our regular mat chats, instructors talk with students about noticing their inner voice and correcting its course. We also teach students to challenge the negative inner voice, which is filled with unreasonable doubt. To help students develop a positive inner voice, we re-train them to believe the impossible is merely opinion. We focus on building their self-esteem and confidence through challenges and by breaking through their comfort zones. To reinforce a positive mindset, we must reward perseverance and not outcome alone. This encourages students to push on through difficult times and develop a mindset that gives them hope and allows them to push themselves. We call this the black belt mindset.

The gift of a positive mindset – walking again

I'd like to share a personal experience that has shaped my life. I hope you enjoy reading about my recovery and that it explains why I owe my ability to walk again to martial arts.

I'll begin this story in Switzerland. Both feet elevated in temporary casts and dosed up on morphine, I was lying in a bed in Interlaken Hospital. In the stereotypical – almost comical – manner, the surgeon looked over his clipboard and said it:

'I'm sorry, Mr Bates, you won't be walking again.'

If it wasn't for his rather serious expression and sensible tone, I would have assumed the surgeon had a refreshingly sarcastic sense of humour. Unfortunately, he didn't.

It had all started because my father was in the Parachute Regiment in the British Army, and as a young boy I would watch in wonder as he jumped from planes. I always had the itch to skydive and experience free-fall. I signed up for a skydiving course and qualified within a few months. I had become obsessed. Any spare time I had, I spent jumping. Skydiving took me around the world, and I did hundreds of jumps in America. Much like martial arts, in skydiving there is obvious progression and there are many routes you can go down. For me, the next step was learning to fly a wingsuit. Flying a wing-suit was like nothing else – cruising like a bird at 150–200mph, playing with the clouds in the world's biggest playground.

While humans surely aren't designed to do this, it was the most fun I had ever had, and I wanted more. I knew base-jumping was the next step for me. 'Base' stands for four categories of fixed objects from which you can jump: building, antenna, span (bridge or arch) and earth (cliff). The risks were much higher – there's no reserve parachute and more base-jumpers were dying every year. After years of training, hundreds of jumps and a lot more experience, I did my first base jumps off cliffs and bridges in Idaho, USA. I found so many psychological similarities between base-jumping and professional fighting. Calming the mind, trusting yourself, attention to detail and persevering with tech-nique, to name a few.

Base-jumping took me all over Europe for the huge cliffs and inspiring scenery. I soon started wingsuit base-jumping, spending months at a time living and jumping in some remote mountainous locations. It was an incredible life, surrounded by a vibrant and exciting community doing an exhilarating hobby that we were all passionate about. I can recall hundreds of stories from the mountains, abseiling down cliffs, drinking from waterfalls while deer sprinted past me along the sheer cliff, flinging my body off mountains as the sun rose or set in the most beautiful places in the world.

The Japanese have a word, *yugen*, which means 'a profound awareness of the universe that triggers a deep emotional response'. This word encapsulates my time in the mountains. Standing on the edge of a thousand-foot cliff in a wingsuit, my arms were strapped to my sides with just enough space to create a wing. You can imagine it's a similar feeling to being in a straitjacket. You trust your kit and your training. Breathing slowly, bringing my feet over the edge of the cliff, heart pounding, body shaking, it was the seventh jump I had done and the seventh time I had climbed the Via Ferrata to the exit point; the last jump of the day.

With over five hundred jumps, the drills were second nature. I heard my Thai trainer's voice in my head through every jump, saying 'Calm mind'. Counting down from three, looking up at the horizon, one big push and I'm gone…

There's a precise moment between standing on the edge of the cliff and leaning forward to start the jump when there is no going back. When you get to this point, you're totally committed and you need to follow through with absolute confidence – 17 July 2014 was a day that changed it all. The turning point.

Three seconds of dead air, stomach sinking and then, comfortable and in control, I'm at 120mph in a wingsuit. I'm flying past the waterfall on the left, turn into open space above the tree line and pitch the parachute. Parachute opens perfectly – I have twenty seconds until landing. I follow the drills, quickly unzip the left wing, go to unzip the right wing, but there's a problem – the zip's jammed. Suddenly, I'm heading towards power lines. I fall back on muscle memory, taking immediate evasive action, using my right hand to pull left risers down hard to force my body into a 180-degree emergency turn.

The canopy collapses, and I'm falling fifty feet. Time slows down. I'm bringing my feet together to brace for impact and avoid a serious spinal injury.

Impact.

Both feet, both ankles and one leg broken. I later learned that the heel bone completely crumbled and all the ligaments were blown off my left foot. Still conscious, I didn't need to call for help; people heard the thud of my body hitting the ground and were already on the way. A group of French climbers and base-jumpers who had seen me falling rushed over, happy to see I was conscious and alive. So often, that isn't the case. Stuck in the Swiss Alps, the air ambulance was unable to reach me. The only solution was a long, bumpy journey to the hospital by road without morphine.

It took four days for the swelling to go down before they could operate. Confused surgeons stood looking at the blurry X-rays. It was clear that some serious damage had been done. To avoid a £20,000 Swiss operation to put me back together again, I needed to get back to the UK. I was unable to fly, but I remembered my car was parked at the hostel in Lauterbrunnen, only one town away.

I managed to get the word out to the UK. Unfortunately, with an older sister getting married in four days and the house filled with distant relatives gathering for the event, the timing wasn't great. An already stressed family didn't need an emergency. Still, my dad managed to fly out to Switzerland in secret within twenty-four hours. We had managed to convince the doctors that, providing they give me enough blood-thinning medication, injections and morphine for me to take on the trip, I could survive the twenty-hour journey from the Swiss hospital to the British hospital.

This bit wasn't fun. In twenty hours, we cracked it. Plenty of coffee stops helped. We'd been instructed to inject blood thinners into my thigh every four hours. I had never given myself an injection before. I've always hated injections, embarrassingly passing out during vaccinations in school. What I discovered on the journey was that my dad wasn't keen on them either – we laughed for a long time discussing who should do the injecting. In the end, after a few amateur attempts, I managed it. The plan had worked and I was now in the UK hospital awaiting surgery.

The surgery was a success. The loose fragmented bone from the heel was removed, the tendons along both sides of my left foot were reattached. But the English surgeon reiterated what the Swiss surgeon had said. My chances of walking again were slim, I would never walk without a limp and running, jumping or taking part in any competitive martial arts would be impossible. The nerves had been permanently damaged. I was unable to feel my foot or move it. I was told that I would gradually get some of this feeling and movement back, but never as much as before.

It took a while for this to all sink in. My life would never be the same again. That turning point and all the decisions leading up to it burned into my mind. Recovery was going to be long. As a young man of twenty-four, I was meant to be spending the summer in Switzerland and Italy, hiking up mountains with friends and flying down, pushing my body and my mind, seeing wonderful sights and having incredible experiences. Instead, I was stuck horizontal on a sofa bed for three months injecting blood thinners into my leg, trying to stay positive. I had lost all ability to use my left foot. My muscles began wasting away and all professional medical advice from surgeons, physiotherapists and doctors was pessimistic and disheartening. They all agreed what the final outcome would be.

The decision on my future had been made. Yet, I wouldn't accept it. I was convinced I would make a full recovery, and I began to resent anyone who had an opinion about my recovery that did not sit with my own. Some would call it denial, some delusion. There was no other outcome in my mind, no plan B. I knew that in six weeks, my clubs were due to start back up. I had six weeks to be physically able to teach martial arts or I would lose all the clubs that I had worked so hard to build.

Summer is the time when most base-jumpers lose their lives in accidents, as people do more jumps in good weather. Two of the friends I was meant to be jumping with lost their lives that summer – two funerals I couldn't attend. It was a dark time. I asked myself what mattered in my life. Why was I in this position? What was my purpose? Perhaps by preventing me from aggressively pursuing more jumps, the accident had saved my life.

Some things only make sense when you look back at them years later. You can often see a clear route and set of decisions that led you to your current position. The lessons you learned five or ten years ago can prove invaluable later on. For years, I had told the parents of my students to bring their children to class even if they were injured. If they had a broken arm, they could work on their kicks; if they had a broken leg, they could write notes and learn. The words I had been saying to my students for so long were etched into my mind: 'You can always train.'

I was determined to practise what I had preached. My training in martial arts would pull me out of the dark hole I was in. I would walk again and I would teach again.

I bought a library of books online about ankle surgery and recovery, the nervous system and nutrition, reading case study after case study about patients who had recovered from injuries similar to my own. I devised a programme of small steps over the summer and became obsessed with progressing in any way. I did desensitising training to stop the sudden rush of pain from damaged nerves, and flexibility training to get the suppleness in my ankle joints back to a point where I could put my foot down on the floor in the correct position to walk. I began bodyweight training to prevent my muscles from wasting further and causing more problems and imbalances.

Week by week, I started to notice a difference. A few degrees here, a feeling in the toes one morning or more range of motion in the ankle. The training was mind-numbingly boring, painful and repetitive. I was exhausted. Although all seemed lost, I explored new ideas and philosophies to try in my classes and add value to my own organisation. I convinced myself that not only would I go back to teaching full time, but my clubs would grow.

I remember so clearly the day I put weight on my left foot, aided by crutches, still in a cast. My right foot was almost fully recovered, despite long-term tendonitis and wasted muscles. I could bear weight and finally, aided by two crutches, I was walking. I had one week until classes started back up.

In an open letter to the parents of my students, I explained the situation. I continued training hard and turned up to the first class on crutches. I remember a parent opening a door for me as the students looked up at their broken instructor. I taught martial arts for three months on crutches. It would be a learning opportunity for students and instructor.

Through training hard at home, I was able to apply more weight to my left foot. I found myself taking small trips around the house – to the fridge, to the bathroom – unaided by crutches. By focusing on small steps, applying a positive mindset and persevering, I had made steady, hard-won progress.

Indomitable spirit, perseverance, self-control – three of the five tenets of tae kwon do that we ask our students to memorise. Now they were more than memorised words; they were living words, put into action through my recovery. By month six, I was walking with a limp. By month eighteen, I was walking without a limp. The surgeons were wrong. I had done what they said was not possible.

The long recovery had given me plenty of time to read about other martial arts organisations and philosophies and, within the next year and a half, it had paid off. My little organisation of 100 students had grown to 500.

It was clear that professional Muay Thai would never be an option again. I could never compete at such a high level with the serious damage I had done to my tendons and bones. Fortunately, though, I had found something incredible in my recovery. I tested many sports to see what was possible with my injuries, struggling with constant tendonitis and degenerative arthritis. Nothing seemed to work. I needed something with zero impact.

I found a local Brazilian jiu-jitsu club in Bath, and talked with the instructor about my problems. After the first class, I was hooked. I spent two years training every day. The martial arts community, the positivity and the low-impact holistic approach to training created the perfect platform for rehabilitation.

On paper, recovery wasn't possible. Looking back at it, though, and joining up the dots, it's clear that this story begins twenty years ago.

A young boy looking up at his tae kwon do instructor in awe, listening diligently to the teachings of an art that instils values that are carried for life. The focus, determination and perseverance that martial arts had given me had pulled me out of one of the darkest times of my life. And into an incredible new chapter.

Finding inspiration within – your strength is your individuality

> 'If you celebrate your difference, the world will, too. It believes exactly what you tell it – through the words you use to describe yourself, the actions you take to care for yourself, and the choices you make to express yourself. Tell the world you are a one-of-a-kind creation who came here to experience wonder and spread joy. Expect to be accommodated.'
> — *Victoria Moran*
> *Lit From Within: Tending your soul for lifelong beauty*

At the Warrior Academy, we believe each child is unique and they need a unique approach. We like to work on their strengths and develop their breakthrough areas. In essence, martial arts is an individual sport with the benefit of being part of a like-minded, supportive team.

Here's what one parent has shared about martial arts as an alternative to team sports:

For years, schools have put a huge emphasis on team sports. Football, rugby, hockey and netball are taught to boys and girls as standard practice. Some children simply don't suit these team sports – the one lesson in the timetable they dread; the one where their lack of skill stands out; their confidence gets knocked; they feel humiliated, upset or out of place.

Ask a bunch of adults their memories of PE and you'll probably find the majority hated it and, as a result, continue to fear 'sport' for the rest of their lives. Then you have the handful who loved it and were picked to play for every team, the apple of the PE teacher's eye.

Thankfully clubs like the Warrior Academy are coming to our schools and bringing this to an end. It introduces children to a whole new kind of sport – one where they can work alone, but within a group of like-minded friends, and progress at their own rate. Not to say it doesn't involve teamwork, but it allows kids to take themselves on their own journey without the pressure of an overbearing teammate or frightening performance against mismatched opponents. My son loves his martial arts class; he looks forward to a grading knowing that he's there because he's earned the right to be there, not to make up numbers in the five-a-side.

He respects the instructors while having so much fun that he can't wait to show me his 'ninja moves' after each class. It's given him a quiet confidence that he can do sport as well as the classmate who captains the A team in football. This kind of experience is invaluable and I'm determined to spread the word about the huge benefits of martial arts and other individual sports that haven't made it into the school timetable... yet!'

Liddy, parent of a Warrior Academy student

Strengths and weaknesses – an exercise

We teach our students that black belts are all unique. We all have different strengths and weaknesses, but we must have a strong sense of self-worth. Discovering who we are and what we are brilliant at can fill us with positivity and develop our sense of self. This can give us the inspiration to achieve greatness.

Young students are so motivated to conform and be like one another so they don't stand out as a potential target for bullying or social rejection, and yet so much power is unleashed from being individual and unique. As students develop within our programme, from a skill-based point of view we encourage individuality, especially in sparring or patterns where students can develop their style. Through developing their own style, they develop their unique character.

I've included a short but powerful exercise that we use to encourage our students to highlight their differences and unique gifts and talents. When students understand their own uniqueness, they find inspiration intrinsically.

Your child should do part one of this exercise alone, and part two in a group or as a pair.

EXERCISE

Part one

A: List your strengths. Write down any small thing you believe you are good at. Be as broad as you can.

Example:

– I'm good at drawing, I'm good at typing quickly, I'm good at making people laugh with jokes and my sense of humour.

B: List your weaknesses. To truly get to know ourselves, we must know our strong and weak points.

Example:

– I can sometimes be lazy in the morning, I often interrupt a lot during conversations, I rush my homework.

Part two

In pairs or in a group, answer the following questions about the other person. Do this in private. You will swap your answers afterwards.

A: What skills do you think your friend has and is really good at?

Example:

– Sarah has neat handwriting and in netball she's very flexible and can run really fast.

B: What makes them special and unique?

Example:

– Sarah is always smiling and happy. She's good at helping people when they're upset. She's brilliant at cheering people up and helping them through tough times. Sarah has a positive mindset and doesn't give up.

In my experience, the answers students give about themselves are rarely an accurate or full representation of who they are and what they are brilliant at. This exercise helps highlight other areas where they shine, which gives them an excellent insight they can use when developing their sense of self.

Let's wrap it up

In this chapter we have explored the importance for young people of regular inspiration, and of effective mentoring, and introduced the concept of 'black belt mentoring'. I've also shared the story of how I overcame a life threatening accident, and how I believe it was martial arts that gave me the tools to walk again and fight through four years of rehabilitation. We have discussed the power of martial arts as a solution for individuals who are seeking something outside of traditional team sports. Finally, we've examined how our individuality can be an inspiration. The brief exercise aims to illuminate the areas we shine in as individuals.

CHAPTER SEVEN

Black Belt Confidence

What is black belt confidence?

A person with black belt confidence is someone who:

- Constantly takes themselves out of their comfort zone

- Has an aura of confidence

- Is proficient in public speaking

- Has a strong sense of pride

- Has learnt to overcome their own fears and challenges

- Has developed strong leadership skills using their own experiences

In the Warrior Method programme, we talk to our students and parents about developing black belt confidence. Part of the reason we describe each part of the black belt mindset using the term 'black belt' is to put the development of the mind into context and make the concept more 'concrete' so students can visualise what it means. It also ensures the physical black belt that students wear is not necessarily the big goal. It's also the values that make up their character: black belt confidence, conduct and concentration.

To make black belt confidence achievable, we break it down into small steps that young people can take gradually. We break the goals down into yearly, monthly, weekly and daily goals. This is combined with constant positive reinforcement and peer support, instilling a strong mindset that sees opportunity in the world and encourages students to go out of their comfort zone, and building the skills needed to pass their knowledge on to other students.

Develop black belt confidence in your child

Having taught thousands of children and mentored them through challenging times, I have seen many young people transform their lives by improving their confidence. With that in mind, confidence is something I'm passionate about developing in our students. Practising martial arts can quickly develop confidence in children, and the Warrior Method is a powerful tool for doing so.

Confidence is one of the most important values we pass on to our young students. Low confidence affects everything in life – from our aspirations, work life and the enjoyment we take from life to our relationships with family, friends, partners and children. If we have a strong sense of self and a high level of confidence, we are more likely to achieve things that will bring us happiness and improve their lives of others. We are more likely to step out of our comfort zone, make a difference and tackle challenges head on without hesitating.

The comfort zone

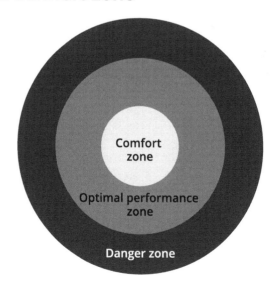

The comfort zone is the psychological state in which we feel the least amount of stress and anxiety. It's where we feel the most in control and the least vulnerable.

Brené Brown, a research professor at the University of Houston, explains the comfort zone as a place 'where our uncertainty, scarcity and vulnerability are minimized – where we believe we'll have access to enough love, food, talent, time, admiration. Where we feel we have some control.'[17]

By understanding the comfort zone, we can use it to our advantage. As we learn the process of controlling our anxiety and fear, our confidence grows. It's inspiring to see the compounding effect of our positive, courageous decisions.

As an extreme sports enthusiast, a professional fighter and a big fan of adventure in general, I believe stepping out of the comfort zone is vital for growth. As a mentor, performance coach and martial arts instructor I believe we can dramatically improve any person's mindset and quality of life by helping them take small steps outside their comfort zone.

Whenever we step out of our comfort zone, it generates a stress response. That releases adrenaline, which enhances our concentration and focus and puts us in

---

17   www.nytimes.com/2011/02/12/your-money/12shortcuts.html

a state to prepare for the activity we are about to put ourselves through. Depending on where our comfort zone lies (and we can change this with training), standing up to give a speech in front of a few hundred people can create more stress than jumping from a 1,500-foot cliff with a parachute. Not all fear is created equal, and in many cases fear of social rejection can be stronger than fear of injury. We'll look at this later, for now it's important to understand that the comfort zone can be very different from one person to another, so any training should reflect that.

Robert Yerkes, an American psychologist best known for his work in intelligence testing and in the field of comparative psychology, reported, 'Anxiety improves performance until a certain optimum level of arousal has been reached. Beyond that point, performance deteriorates as higher levels of anxiety are attained. Beyond the optimum performance zone, lies the "danger zone" in which performance declines rapidly under the influence of greater anxiety.'[18]

When we are forced to make a decision in the danger zone, we're more likely to make a poor choice and focus on fewer alternatives. We use strategies that we're familiar with and have used before, even if they aren't particularly helpful. With this in mind, it's important that we understand how to reach this

18 Bardwick, JM (1995). *Danger in the Comfort Zone: From Boardroom to Mailroom – How to break the entitlement habit that's killing American business.* Nashville, TN: Amacom.

'optimal performance zone' (or 'high-performance zone') without entering the 'danger zone'. There's a fine line between these zones, and that line moves as we grow and develop.

Regularly stepping out of our comfort zone does a whole host of fantastic things to develop us:

- It dramatically improves our confidence, which is vital for our growth and creates more opportunity in our lives

- It teaches us to make decisions in stressful situations, which develops our leadership ability

- It teaches us to control the mind and stay calm in stressful situations

- As we expand our comfort zone, we seek out more challenges and become more goal orientated

- It can bring us adventure, experiences and enrich our lives

Look at the diagram of the comfort zone and imagine yourself sitting in the small circle – the comfort zone – reading this book. Now imagine yourself in front of a large audience of 2,000 people, reading this paragraph out loud, live on national TV. There is no room for error. At this stage you're likely to have left your comfort zone. As we push ourselves out of the comfort zone and into the optimal performance zone, our stress levels increase and our 'fight or flight' reaction is triggered. We either rush back into the comfort zone ('flight') or we 'fight' through the immediate stress, make bold decisions and stay in the optimal performance zone. The next time we go into the optimal performance zone, we are able to deal with the stress more efficiently. What was previously uncomfortable has become familiar, and we have expanded our comfort zone. In other words, the next time you're on live TV, it shouldn't be quite so terrifying.

As part of the Warrior Method, we teach our students about public speaking. It's a practical skill they will need in their adult lives and developing this skill has a powerful effect on their mindset, confidence, leadership and ability to inspire their fellow students. Let's look at an example of public speaking in one of our martial arts classes to show how we can use the comfort zone to develop black belt confidence.

A child is absolutely terrified of speaking in front of a group of their peers. The instructor encourages the child to stand next to him, in front of all the other students, and shout out the numbers one to five while the group performs a front kick off the back leg. This simple exercise brings the student into their optimal performance zone: they are out of their comfort zone but they are not in 'danger'. The task of counting from one to five is simple enough that the child does not need to rely on any complex decision making while in a stressful situation. Once the child has finished, a big round of applause is given, the child bows and returns to their peers, task completed.

The next time we ask the child to go out, the instructor asks the child to go to the front on their own and shout the numbers out. This is followed with a bow and a round of applause to strengthen the positive experience and give the child social recognition. The next time, the instructor asks the child to describe the kick or use an alternative kick. This is again followed by social recognition in the form of applause.

The time after that, the instructor asks the child to present a complicated combination of three or four techniques, describe what they are teaching and correct anyone in the group who makes a mistake. The child shouts out one to five as usual and the task ends with applause. The child is also rewarded with a leadership stripe on their belt for their progress to give them pride in their leadership.

After this, as part of their grading the child is asked to deliver the same mini-lesson in front of twenty parents and twenty of their peers in exam conditions. This is concluded with applause from the whole room and an award for excellent leadership.

Looking back at where we have come with this child, we can see they have achieved a huge amount of growth by taking mini steps out of their comfort zone and into the optimal performance zone.

The key is to make the most of the young person's optimal performance zone. I believe strong mentoring, excellent peer-group support and positive reinforcement achieve this. With regular visits to the optimal performance zone so that it doesn't become a stranger, students begin to feel comfortable with feeling uncomfortable.

Why it works

All the parents who responded to our survey in 2017 said that they saw an increase in confidence in their children. When comparing confidence levels before and after being in our programme, the average increase was 26%. That's staggering considering that as students grow older many of them have a sudden drop in confidence – for example, due to the stress of adolescence.

Here's why learning martial arts is powerful for developing confidence.

Learning self-defence is empowering. It has an impact on the development of confidence, as young people feel more able to handle a stressful situation, avoid conflict and defend themselves and their loved ones if necessary.

Developing fitness levels improves confidence. When young people feel fit, strong and healthy, they are not as self-conscious about their weight and they are able to take part in other team sports effectively, often excelling. This is thanks to the excellent strength, flexibility and cardiovascular fitness that martial arts provides.

Better focus helps to improve school grades. Young people can carry over the higher level of focus that they develop through into their school work. When their grades go up, so does their confidence.

A strong sense of community improves confidence. Being part of such a supportive network of friendly, like-minded peers who are passionate about the same thing boosts young people's confidence.

Achieving goals improves self-worth. The belt system used in most martial arts creates clear goals for students. By achieving them, they receive constant recognition for their hard work and regular confidence boosts.

Building on leadership skills is empowering. Developing leadership skills teaches students to take control of situations and trust their own judgement. By doing this, they gain masses of confidence.

Let's wrap it up

In this section of the book, I've looked at why inspiring young people is so important, how it opens their eyes to possibilities and how it helps them see the big picture and build their confidence.

I've talked about what we define as black belt mentoring, the importance of curiosity for our future lives and how inspiration increases curiosity. I've discussed the inner voice and the development of a black belt mindset and looked at why our individuality is a strength. Through case studies and stories, I've shown you how students who have been inspired have gone on to achieve great things. I've talked about the comfort zone and why it's important to challenge students to step outside this into the optimal performance zone.

I believe courage earns confidence. Saying this out loud before students compete, take up a challenge or leave their comfort zone gives them a real sense of what it is they will achieve through their actions. By teaching the process of earning confidence, students become inspired by their actions and act as an inspiration to other children in their class.

PART FOUR
THE WARRIOR METHOD – CHALLENGE

CHAPTER EIGHT

Adventure

My introduction to adventure

From a young age, I have had a passion for adventure – a thirst for travel, exploration and conquering challenges.

It's easy for me to trace this back. My father was keen to encourage and reinforce this adventurous spirit. He would regularly go on exercises with the army, living away for four to six months at a time. Although it was always sad to see him leave, we would write to him with 'blueys'. I would be so excited to receive one of these blue letters in the military post – they were sometimes the only contact I had with my dad for months. In these letters and when he got back, he would tell us his amazing stories. He would always tell them as if they were an adventure, although, of course, that may have been far from the reality in Bosnia, Iraq and Northern Ireland. The tales of training in the Belize jungle or in the Arctic would fascinate me. He would come home with a small gift for each of us four kids, a tarantula or knife from the jungle, perhaps – always something exciting.

We lived in Aldershot, which was the home of the Parachute Regiment. I'd watch my dad jump out of planes most weekends. I would point to the sky and ask my older sister which one was Dad. With 200 paras falling from the sky it would have been an incredible feat to know which one he was, but she was always pretty certain.

My years as a young boy in Aldershot were the best of my childhood. If I wasn't in school, I was outside. I spent most of my time climbing in and out of tanks, climbing cargo nets, racing through assault courses and exploring local forests. One day, much to my mother's despair, my dad taught me to abseil down from the top of the garage. I was six years old and in my element. It all ended safely with a new skill learnt, although perhaps it wasn't a typical skill for a boy of that age to pick up. Looking back, it's hard to say if my thirst for adventure was nature or nurture. Certainly, these years in Aldershot planted the seed in my mind that adventure was a high priority in my life. This was solidified by the positive reinforcement from my dad.

From my experiences as a young boy, I was certain I'd be joining the army. But when we moved to Bradford on Avon in Wiltshire, things quickly changed. There were few kids my age in the area, and my dad's work was no longer on an exciting paras' base. I picked up martial arts at age seven and it became my life. It became my whole community and it gave me direction and purpose. I've already talked about how it guided me through difficult transitions, including school changes and bullying. I began competing in martial arts around the UK, won several national titles and became a second degree black belt. My dad was always there to support me at competitions, camcorder in hand so we could analyse each match afterwards. We would often drive for six hours to a competition, only for me to lose in the first match (one-minute rounds) and come home empty-handed. It was always framed as a positive experience, and just leaving the house to go and compete in the Nationals was an adventure with my dad.

As a teenager (ages fourteen and fifteen), I was strongly encouraged to be part of anything adventurous and so naturally I put my name forward for the Ten Tors. This is a thirty-five mile trek across Dartmoor in one and a half days, camping halfway. The smallest in the group and with a heavy bag, I found the whole experience incredibly tough, but I thoroughly enjoyed the challenge and the teamwork. Navigating our way across Dartmoor in terrible conditions was made bearable by the incredible camaraderie my team developed. We felt part of a small, elite group of adventurists. I felt immense pride when we completed the event, coming third out of 400 other school teams. Little did I know that within ten years I would have created an import business to supply all the kit and merchandise to the army for their Ten Tors events.

At age seventeen I would be able to join the Royal Marines Reserves. I couldn't possibly wait until I had finished school, so doing my A levels at the same time seemed like a good decision. The application process began at age sixteen, and the interviews and fitness assessments took half a year. On the week of my seventeenth birthday, I began training. Every week we trained in Bristol, and every other weekend we trained in Lympstone, the home of the Royal Marines. At this point I was still learning to drive so that I could go alone on the hour and a half's journey to Bristol after school each week. For the first six months my dad would come home from work, drive me to Bristol, wait in the car and drive me back, again showing incredible support for any adventurous pursuit.

The training with the Reserves was incredibly difficult. The Commando course was the hardest thing I had ever done. Although I was fit and strong for a young seventeen-year-old, I lacked the stamina of the older guys. I'd come first in the circuit training and assault courses, but I struggled to run for more than six to ten miles with heavy kit, webbing and rifle after a weekend of revising for my A levels and little sleep.

During this time, my grandmother died of Alzheimer's. It was a difficult time for the whole family, and my dad and I decided to raise money for the Alzheimer's Society. We planned what was to be a mad adventure. We packed our mountain bikes into cardboard boxes and shipped them to Marrakech in Morocco. After meeting up with a few ex-army friends who were joining us, we were driven by minibus, with our bikes strapped to the roof, five hundred miles away into the Sahara Desert. We then cycled back through the Sahara, over the Atlas Mountains and down into Marrakech. We each carried twenty litres of water and camping kit. At night, we slept in dry river beds. At seventeen years old, this was quite possibly the most exciting thing I had ever done. We raised thousands of pounds for the Alzheimer's Society and came home with countless stories of struggle and triumph – punctures, running out of water and food and dodging scorpions, to name a few.

At age eighteen I was still training in the Royal Marines Reserves. The weekends were long and packed with tough physical exercise (assault courses, yomping across Dartmoor) and technical classes on shooting, ironing, washing, navigation and so on. I would come into school exhausted on Monday morning and my IT teacher, who taught my first class of the week, became quite concerned because I was sleeping at the back of the class every single Monday.

Being part of the Royal Marines while handling my AS and A level revision and exams was tough. I had to fit in training during the day, running with webbing during each of my free slots in school to build up my stamina. Doing all this while other students were relaxing or catching up on work added a lot of pressure to what most students would consider the hardest academic years of their young lives. Eventually, something had to give and I decided to give up the Royal Marines Reserves. It was a difficult decision, but I was happy and proud to have been on such an incredible adventure and it gave me a real taste of the military. I'd made some great friends and I learnt the importance of camaraderie and the four elements of the Commando spirit: courage, determination, unselfishness and cheerfulness in the face of adversity. The importance of attention to detail was drilled into me regularly during the training. The lessons I learnt were invaluable, and I look back on learning them with fond memories.

The adventures I had up to the age of eighteen, and the lessons they taught me, would determine how I lived my life. Certainly the more extreme adventures I took part in as an adult all stemmed from these younger years. Living a life of adventure has given me so many rich experiences: I have felt every emotion, travelled around the world, found out about many different cultures, and picked up useful skills that have really helped me thrive in this exciting world.

How adventure develops character

Being encouraged to be adventurous from a young age taught me to be creative, resourceful, independent and eager to take up challenges. It also taught me the importance of teamwork, camaraderie, attention to detail and being organised. Every adventure took me outside my comfort zone, so I spent many years jumping in and out of the optimal performance zone we talked about in chapter 7.

The definition of adventure in the Oxford Dictionary focuses on the experience of the individual: 'An unusual and exciting or daring experience'. It's these exciting experiences that shape who we are and the decisions we make. I believe it's important to have them from a young age if we are to thrive in our adult years. In fact, this is another area in which ancient wisdom offers us solutions: the intention behind many of the rituals – some dangerous, all demanding in some way – adolescents must pass through in other societies is for the individuals involved to develop maturity and resilience, demonstrating that they are ready to start the transition to adulthood.

As we get older, the lessons learnt through adventure become even more valuable and vital to our success.

Running out of water in the Sahara Desert while on an old mountain bike with a puncture may be at the extreme end of adventure for many teenagers, but it taught me about resourcefulness and creativity in a stressful situation. The ability to think quickly and to solve a problem can give an adult security and resilience in their personal life and success in their work life.

Camaraderie and being cheerful in the face of adversity can bring out leadership qualities in us that raise team morale and ensure their success in a project or event. Developing these skills through difficult or challenging experiences can help us through difficult personal times – through injury, separation or even loss.

Nothing to fear but fear itself

I'm trying to slow down my breathing.

It's 5am and at this high altitude the air is cold. I take a big breath in and out. I can feel my body shaking, my knees moving forward and backward as I try to stand still in the snow, trying to keep in control.

I'm not shaking because of the temperature. I'm shaking because my nervous system is producing chemicals to mobilise my organs and energy stores to flee a stressor – essentially, gearing my body up for 'fight or flight'.

You see, at this moment in time, I'm standing on the edge of a cliff and two inches in front of me is a drop of 3,000 feet. On my back I have a parachute, and to my left is a friend who is going through the same process as me. I'm balancing on one foot, and it's proving difficult. This is a simple task when you're at sea level, and it should be no different on the edge of a cliff. But two things make this infinitely harder: 1) the chemical warfare going on in my body, which is the physical symptom of 2) the psychological warfare going on in my mind.

To be in this position, ready to perform confidently at such a high level, took years of hard work and meticulous training. It involved hundreds of skydives in preparation, and detailed study of turbulence, angles of attack, glide ratios and packing parachutes, all of which needed masses of attention to detail and focus. Alongside the physical training comes the mental training needed to overcome fear. We are not born courageous or brave, but we can learn. It's nurture, not nature.

On my journey I developed a process to deal with fear and cope with 'fight or flight'. By controlling my mind I could control the physical symptoms of being terrified.

While standing on one foot I'm breathing the cold air in, filling my lungs and exhaling slowly. I'm looking at the horizon. It's a beautiful sunrise in the north of Italy on the snow-capped cliffs of Monte Brento. I fill my mind with an overwhelming sense of gratitude that I am able to feel and experience something so few people have in such a beautiful natural environment. I teach my mind to be calm. To have no thought other than the simple task of standing in this position, in the same way we teach our students to focus solely on their breathing during meditation.

A few more breaths and the shaking stops. I go over my drills. Check chest strap, leg straps, helmet strap. I'm ready. I look to my partner. Three, two, one… jump. A deep breath in, slowly released as we both glide through the dead air, building up speed and moving into a tracking position where we can control the movement of our bodies. I arch, deploy the parachute and the canopy opens with a huge 'thwack', a reassuring sound.

I have always found fear fascinating. It's something we all feel and face, some of us more regularly than others. Its intensity depends on where we are in our comfort zone. From my experience, the fear doesn't ever go away, but it's possible to learn how to deal with it. We can tolerate a higher level of stress and control our fear by getting to know that fear and understanding that it's there to help us – to prepare us to be more alert and improve our reactions. Much like controlling a fire, we need to make sure it doesn't escalate and get out of hand.

Though what we fear varies so wildly, from doing a bungee jump to giving a speech at a wedding, learning to deal with fear – developing a process to help us through it – can have a profound effect on how we face the challenges in our lives.

Conquering fear

In the context of martial arts, we teach students to cope with fear and to take up challenges. This important part of our character-development programme affects their whole life.

Cognitive behavioural therapy (CBT) is a two-pronged approach to deal with phobias that is often used by clinical psychologists. In CBT, participants first deal with their thoughts and attitudes about a specific fear. Then they control the physical response to fear. To teach students how to deal with fear, we combine the CBT approach with meditation and understanding the comfort zone, along with mantras like 'courage earns confidence'.

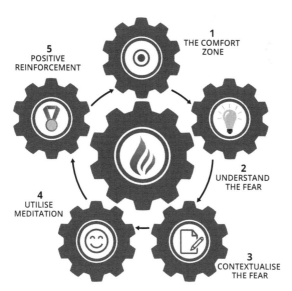

Step one: Understand the importance of the comfort zone

Before we can ask a student to do the thing that they fear, whether that's competing, public speaking or leading a class, we must teach them about the importance of stepping out of their comfort zone. We try to make this tangible with our mantra 'courage earns confidence'. We explain the great benefits of confidence and ask them how it would feel to be someone who can lead the class, compete or speak in public without fear. For example, what emotions would they feel instead? Would they feel proud?

From here we explain that by showing courage they earn confidence – confidence that will allow them to feel those positive emotions and get their 'prize'. We try to make the conversation visual, and we use meditation techniques to bring this image to life. The more visual you can make this step, the more of a driving force you will create for the child.

Step two: Understand your fear

Step two focuses on the individual fear. We look deeply into the worst-case scenario. What's the worst that could possibly happen? What is the most terrible outcome of doing the thing that you fear? Humans have powerful imaginations: our creativity is certainly one of our greatest strengths.

What this imagination also does for us, unfortunately, is exaggerate our fear into a monster that consumes our minds. By adding logic in this moment and diving deep into the details of what could rationally go wrong, we humanise the fear and the monster becomes less of a threat. It begins to become something we may be able to conquer.

Step three: Contextualise the fear

Next it's time to put the fear into perspective. We do this by placing it next to far greater fears out there (appropriate to the student's age) – for example, fear of social rejection, fear of death, injury or loss. When we place our fear next to these examples, it feels insignificant. The monster we have created in our minds becomes less daunting.

Step four: Step, meditate, step, meditate

At this stage, many students are capable of jumping straight in and doing the thing that they fear. Where possible, we have found it's incredibly beneficial to strengthen the learning experience by taking a small step or doing part of the challenge first. Students then go back to meditate on the three steps above before taking another step.

Step five: Immediate positive reinforcement

With positive reinforcement, it's best to 'strike while the iron's hot': immediately reward the student while they're at the apex of the emotions they feel from doing the thing that they fear will put the whole experience into a positive light straight away. In class, we achieve this by giving a big round of applause or by giving an award for perseverance or leadership in front of everyone. This public recognition creates a strong association with positive feelings and being in the optimal performance zone.

By following this method of overcoming fear, our students in the Warrior Academy have conquered their inner demons. In many cases, the thing they feared the most becomes the thing they enjoy the most. We rewire the way they think about challenges. This has a huge effect on their personal development and is a practical tool they can use in their adult life.

Let's wrap it up

We all feel fear, but a person who is equipped with a system or process to conquer their fears is a more confident individual. They can go on to do challenging things in their life without being held back by the fear of failure or rejection. As adults, many of us never reach our full potential because we lack confidence or fear rejection, failure or loss. Inevitably, we miss out on the beauty of life, and we show this fear of loss by not challenging ourselves to overcome our fear.

Some of the stories of adventure I have shared are at the extreme end of the spectrum. When teaching children about challenges and tackling fear, these stories are not always relevant or appropriate. Though we all have different comfort zones, the process of overcoming fear is always the same and can be applied to anyone.

As part of this step – challenge – I have talked about the importance of adventure and breaking through the comfort zone. It's now time to delve deep into the how, what and why of challenge. In the next chapter I will talk about competition and its importance in the development of character.

CHAPTER NINE

Competition

Why competition is important

I've talked in depth about how adventure can encourage our students to explore, learn about life and develop. I've looked at the comfort zone and how fear is a process we can overcome. In this chapter I'll look at how competition is vital to the development of a black belt character in young people. I'll also explore how success and failure are both important learning experiences for young people.

In today's world, competition is often discouraged in schools. I believe this is because it is taken out of context, so failure is seen as a damaging part of the learning environment. In my opinion, the opposite is true. I believe that students who learn to compete in a healthy, positive way are more likely to contribute to the community, as they will have developed important leadership skills and will be far more likely to support their peers or teammates, helping them through difficult times.

Adult life is pretty tough. It's packed full of ups and downs: stress, disappointment, joy, elation and hard work. Taking competition out of the syllabus for young people deprives them of important life lessons. Because of the diversity of adult life, learning what it's like to succeed and learning what it's like to fail are equally important. Learning what can go right or wrong, and gaining the tools to overcome adversity, will help them in their adult years.

It's true that for many students, competing in sport or academically isn't motivating. In fact, the thought of competing against their peers can completely put them off a subject or a class. I believe that with careful management of 'competition', this can be overcome.

A successful programme that helps a young person grow and develops their character will cater for their unique needs. On the one hand, a professional character-building programme will cater for the student who wants to pursue elite-level competition, competing against their peers and others in the community at a national or even international level. On the other hand, such a programme should provide a structure for developing a competitive spirit in students who want to avoid competing against peers. This can be achieved through competing with oneself – where students are achieving personal bests or individual goals, developing themselves to improve on a previous version of themselves.

In short, a professional character-development programme should cater for those who want to be at the top of the game, while also providing the tools needed to compete with oneself to achieve personal goals. Eradicating the concept of competition purely to avoid disappointment is damaging.

Martial arts focuses on the individual. It's a powerful tool for personal development. A student can set and achieve competitive goals to better themselves without the influence of peers. Meanwhile, they're supported by a community and can enjoy the feeling of being 'part of a team'. This concept is certainly hard to find outside martial arts communities.

Discovering your child's motivation

To truly overcome challenges and help guide students to develop a strong mindset, we must discover their motivation. To find out what motivates your child, it's important to talk with them. In my experience, many teachers and parents find discovering their students' or child's motivation difficult because of a communication gap, rather than a generation gap.

First, ask what your student or child likes about a sport, club or class. Try to discover how they feel when they are taking part in each aspect of the activity. How do they feel when something goes well? The answers will be different for each person. As you discover the factors that motivate them, do you see a pattern? Is there a clear motivator? Often, a strong motivating factor is appreciation or recognition. Keeping these in mind, ask how the child feels when things go wrong and try to find out the best way to overcome these negative feelings.

As a coach or mentor it's so important to understand the root of a student's motivation or drive – their 'why'. With this information it's far easier to encourage and help them through difficult, challenging times.

How we run competitions and develop personal goals

Martial arts focus on the individual, which is powerful for personal development. As I mentioned earlier, in martial arts students can set and achieve competitive goals to better themselves, without the influence of peers, while being supported by a community and nurturing the feeling of being part of a team.

Some excellent examples of personal goals that promote individual competition in the Warrior Academy classes are:

- Learning a new pattern or combination

- Earning my next stripe or belt

- Doing more reps on a fitness exercise (press-ups, squat jumps and so on)

In Warrior Academy clubs we cater for students who enjoy competing with others and seek to test their skills in a public, competitive environment. To help these students we run in-house Warrior Academy competitions, which are specially designed to hold four categories of competition (patterns, point stop, continuous sparring and board breaking). We split students into smaller groups so they have a high chance of building up 'small wins' and to make the experience less daunting. This method ensures students gain valuable competition experience throughout the day, which is different from the typical 'sudden death' style of competition that large tournaments are known for.

The fundamental goal here is to develop students' understanding of important life lessons like success, failure and supporting their peers. This does an excellent job of bridging the gap between personal development and public competition.

For students who wish to go on to compete at the elite level, we invite students to national competitions to truly test their skills and mindset.

Thanks for a fantastic competition today. You create this lovely family atmosphere where the children can try out their skills in a really supportive environment. Joe sets himself very high standards and gets very frustrated with himself, but his reaction today was much improved from the last one so this was great to see. Yet again you guys took very good care of him and noticed when he was struggling. He decided not to do the Ultimate Warrior because, as he said, 'I am very happy with my performance and don't want to spoil it by getting upset at the end!' I was really proud of his mature approach and he is now at home watching the videos I took and working out where he could improve.

Where he has come from over the last few years is amazing and that has been undoubtedly helped by the great work you guys have done with him and your patient and supportive ethos. I feel very lucky that we found the Warrior Academy – it has given him a sporting framework which has really helped him develop, and I was also really proud to see him coaching Harley in the weapons competition today.

Rachael, mother of Joe

Support from parents is vital to developing this kind of black belt spirit. Following two excellent Warrior competitions and a huge amount of dedication to perfecting his skills, Joe is now going on to compete in the English Championships.

What is failure?

From the age of five I was competing regularly in martial arts, and I was also failing regularly. My dad would take me to competitions all around the country, often driving for many hours. The fear, pressure and anticipation I felt was often extremely difficult to control. The disappointment of losing within the first minute in a sudden death tournament and having to make the long journey home with no medal or trophy was hard to overcome. Fortunately, my dad was always supportive. He never seemed disappointed – instead, he used the loss as an opportunity to pass on life lessons in perseverance that would help me overcome my weaknesses.

This is an excellent method for helping a young person develop, and it certainly helped to shape my character in the right way. As I progressed I began to compete more often, and the fear and nerves began to subside. I was winning national competitions in several organisations every year. Eventually, as an adult I went on to train and fight professionally, full contact, in other martial arts around the world.

I believe we learn far more through failure than through success, as long as failure is put into the right context and the child receives excellent mentoring. Martial arts, taught professionally as part of a progressive character-development programme, can develop a competitive spirit in young people. This spirit will guide them through difficult times and prepare them for adult life. Instead of teaching young people to avoid competition, let's put competition, success and failure in a context that will help them develop a strong character.

Analysing performance positively

To develop an unshakable black belt mindset and the ability to overcome failure in a mature and positive way, we need four things:

- Experience of success and failure

- A strong mentor

- A supportive community

- A process for analysing performance

Before we can develop a black belt mindset and learn to analyse our performance, we need to have the opportunity to perform. That means challenging ourselves – or competing – is an important first step. At Warrior Academy we always start with personal challenges that focus on self-improvement before we introduce students to public competition. We need to build the foundation first.

It's important that students have a strong mentor who can see them through each phase from beginning to end. The bond between instructor and student is powerful, and trust must be developed. Without a mentor and the development of trust, it's harder for a student to work through difficult times or overcome particularly tough failures. They're also likely to waste learning opportunities from a successful experience if they don't analyse their performance.

It's vital that the student has a supportive community before, during or after they compete (if possible, at all three times). If the student is successful, the community will solidify that success and publicly recognise the achievement, reinforcing the positive experience. In times of failure, the community will provide a friendly, nurturing environment where the student feels emotionally supported and does not feel judged. This will help them to bounce back.

I've put the Warrior process for analysing performance into an exercise called the Four Rs, which you can use to analyse performance after a competition or challenge. This process will help your child or student develop from failure or success by using it as a powerful learning experience. Remember, both failure and success give us the opportunity to grow.

Following the steps set out in the exercise helps to develop a black belt mindset. This is a strong mindset that enables a student to tune in to their own performance, overcome defeat or failure and learn from every experience. As students develop more, they realise that growth in mindset is not a linear process. It takes time to develop the principles, but once they are in place students show a sharp rise in their development towards a black belt mindset.

The Four Rs

01 REWARD
Having a planned reward to give them immediately after a competition or event will solidify the event as a positive experience.

02 RECOVER
Competing is both emotionally and physically draining; a planned period of recovery is essential.

03 REGROUP
Re-grouping covers analysing your performance and technique, getting back into your community, supporting your peers and setting new goals.

04 REPEAT
We grow when we compete and the more we gain experience in competition the more confident we become. Begin your new challenge!

I've created the Four Rs – reward, recover, regroup, repeat – to use immediately after a student competes or performs a challenge.

Step one: Reward

Regardless of the outcome, have a planned reward in place. (Some of the rewards our students have chosen include a trip to the cinema or the beach, a meal out in a favourite restaurant, and a movie night at home.) It can take great courage for a young person to compete or attempt a challenge. Rewarding them immediately after a competition or event will solidify the event as a positive experience. For this reason, you should give a reward no matter whether the outcome is successful or not. I believe it is important to have a hierarchy in the way awards are presented in competitions: if students understand that there is a greater reward for winning, this will drive their competitive spirit, increase their motivation and develop their character. In a competition, there are usually medals or trophies for first, second and third place. Parents and peers should provide support immediately before (in the build-up phase), during (at the event) and after the competition. The support after the event should take the form of a planned reward – win or lose.

Step two: Recover

Competing is emotionally and physically draining. The build-up to a single event might have been going on for months. All the worries, frustrations, pressures, hopes and dreams about the outcome can build up to an apex of emotions on the day, which can be incredibly draining for a young person. Encourage them to take some time off afterwards. At this stage, they should spend this time relaxing and recovering rather than reflecting on the competition. Let them enjoy a calm mind and a quiet sense of pride, with no thoughts of upcoming competitions.

Step three: Regroup

This is an important step. Regrouping is when a young person analyses their performance and technique and sets new goals. Let's dive into how to structure each aspect of regrouping using the Warrior Method.

Analyse performance. First, guide the young person through the whole process they faced, looking closely at their build-up, their event and how they felt. This helps them gain a deep understanding of the competition cycle. We find that discussing the following questions, guiding students through them one by one, helps.

Before the event:

- How did you feel going into the competition?

- Did you have a positive mindset leading up to the competition?

- Would you change your mindset leading up to the competition?

- Did you find the competition to be challenging and out of your comfort zone?

During the event:

- Do you feel you gave your best performance in the competition?

- Looking back, what would you improve about your technique (even if you feel that it was brilliant)?

After the event:

- What advice would you give to your friends and peers who are going to the same competition?

- How can you help others in your community prepare for a similar competition?

- How did you feel after the competition? Did you feel pride, relief, happiness?

- How can you prepare better for your next competition?

- Do you have another goal you would like to achieve?

- Who do you need to thank for helping you prepare for the competition and for supporting you?

As a mentor, it's vital to analyse performance in a positive but honest way to get the best results. Notice that the elements of community and leadership appear in every aspect of the performance analysis. We do this to ensure students remain humble, support each other and understand that we rarely achieve greatness alone. Indeed, our community is fundamental to our success.

Set goals. After analysing the performance, it's time to set new goals. For this part of the exercise, it's important to set goals, breaking down the big vision into smaller, manageable goals and daily habits.

Step four: Repeat

The final step is to encourage the young person to repeat the process of competing and analysing. Encourage them to see competition or challenges not as one-off life events but as a process for learning and applying those lessons. Having goals brings drive and purpose to our lives. Competing challenges us and takes us out of our comfort zone. We grow when we compete: the more we gain experience in competition, the more confident we become. Encourage the young person to carry what they've learned into all areas of their life. As adults, they'll often find themselves in a competitive environment, so plenty of experience competing and a healthy process of analysing their performance can make a big difference to their happiness and success in later life.

Let's wrap it up

In this chapter I've emphasised the importance of competition and its effect on a young person's development. Competition is often discouraged, but this is because it is taken out of context, with failure learned as a damaging component of the learning process, whereas I believe the opposite is true. Failure is a fundamental stepping-stone and a learning opportunity essential for development.

I've discussed how we tailor our competitions to the unique needs of each individual, while providing the supporting framework of our Warrior Family. Students feel as if they are part of a team while essentially competing with themselves. We've examined how vital it is for students to be given the opportunity to really test themselves. Encouraging any form of competition and rewarding courage are important, as is providing access to higher-level competition.

We've looked at failure and the Warrior Academy system for analysing performance positively: the Four Rs – reward, recover, regroup and repeat. This system has helped countless students overcome failure and progress very quickly.

CHAPTER TEN

Setting Goals

Why it's important to set goals

While we expect adults to have goals, we rarely think of a child of four or six with a set of their own goals. Yet goals stem from healthy needs, wants, desires and ambition, all of which we have at any age. Naturally, we each have our own unique goals.

Learning to set and achieve goals helps young people in several ways. It develops their focus, as to achieve each goal they need to set targets and apply themselves in one form or another. The process of setting goals improves their analytical skills as they break down big goals into smaller ones and begin to pick apart the process of success. It also develops their patience, as they learn to delay gratification until they've achieved a goal and can earn a reward. All of this is a healthy learning experience.

Learning to set and achieve their own goals improves young people's self-esteem and confidence. They begin to understand that big goals are in fact easily achievable if they're broken down. The feeling of being rewarded and recognised for their hard work will reinforce the positive feelings that come from making their own success. Learning about setting and achieving goals teaches a child about perseverance, about 'not giving up' – and this will give them drive to succeed.

These valuable learning experiences not only help young people to achieve their goals, but also develop their character.

Reinforcing success with planned rewards

Later in this chapter I'll explain our system for setting and achieving goals in a practical way. First, it's important to understand an essential factor in each goal's success. Reinforcing the successful achievement of a desired outcome will build a relationship in a young person's mind between hard work and positivity.

By planning rewards, we can give young people more motivation to push through difficult times. In turn, this improves their perseverance. When choosing an appropriate reward, it's important to keep it in proportion to the size or difficulty of the goal or challenge.

The goal here is to strengthen the relationship between hard work and a 'prize'. If the reward is the same regardless of the goal, there is no correlation between the amount of work put in and the result. That lack of correlation will have a damaging effect on the goal-setting process. Students will begin to realise they will 'win' no matter what their output is. In many competitions, a medal or award for taking part is a fantastic confidence-builder that reinforces the student's courage to compete. But there must also be a hierarchy in the awards given so the higher achievers get a reward that represents their greater achievement.

Step back and let your ninja pick themselves up

As a young person, your student or child will encounter difficult challenges and tasks. They may sometimes seem mentally drained or physically exhausted, but it's important that we don't come to the rescue every time. If an appropriate system is used, the goal they are set should be within their grasp and shouldn't cause them significant distress.

The young person should have the ability after a period of hardship to overcome the obstacles that have made the goal or challenge difficult. The result will be a more confident and independent child. Of course, seeing your child or student struggling isn't easy, but it's important to keep in mind that without failures and hardships they can't develop their character. It's the lessons learnt in these difficult periods that will help them cope with far more difficult situations as adults.

Instead of feeling that you need to pick your child up, help them set appropriate goals and let them pick themselves up. Be the driving force for motivation, the support net for security and their biggest fan when they achieve.

The Warrior Academy goal-setting system

At the Warrior Academy, we've designed a system of setting goals to help students break down big goals into small chunks – from years to months, weeks, days and daily habits. The aim is for students to learn the process of goal setting so they can achieve this on their own and apply it to every aspect of their life.

The Warrior Academy goal-setting system is based on SMART goals. This concept has been around for a while now, not surprisingly, as SMART goals are extremely effective. SMART stands for specific, measurable, attainable, relevant and time bound.

Specific: By setting a specific goal, we focus the mind on the single task we need to achieve, without being confused or distracted. Specific goals are also easier to measure than general or broader goals.

Measurable: We must be able to measure the success of our work or efforts. This is how we know if the outcome is a success. Typically, our goals are measured in terms of time or frequency, such as number of additional repetitions of an exercise completed, or seconds shaved off a 5km run.

Attainable: In my experience, goals are often too difficult or too easy to achieve. If they're way too big, without being broken down, they're unattainable. While thinking big is excellent, setting one big goal without a plan for achieving it can lead to us losing confidence and motivation. A goal that is too small, which doesn't push us out of our comfort zone in the slightest, won't give us the drive we need to grow. The best type of goal forms part of a bigger plan. It challenges us, but we know that with hard work we can achieve it.

Relevant: The student must decide the goals, and they must make a difference in their own life. With young students, I've found that the goal itself is not as important as learning the process of goal setting. We can encourage this by making the goals relevant to their lives. This also keeps their motivation up.

Time bound: It's important to give a time frame to the goals we set for two main reasons: first, so we can measure progress effectively, and second, so there is a deadline to meet. Without this, our concentration and focus can lapse, and it's unlikely that we will complete a challenging goal. It's also important to give students a suitable amount of time to achieve a goal, as we don't want them to feel overwhelmed and give up.

Many businesses use the SMARTER approach for setting goals. The E and R at the end stand for 'ethical' and 'recorded'. For our purposes, I've found that it's more beneficial to use the E and R as:

Enjoyable: An important part of maintaining motivation is to enjoy the process. Planning fun sessions can keep us on track to pursue our goals.

Rewarding: We must plan a series of rewards for each goal. This solidifies the learning experience.

With SMARTER in place as the backbone for setting goals, at the Warrior Academy we encourage students to follow the eight steps in the exercise below. These help them to decide, break down and evaluate their goals.

EXERCISE

Step one: Identify a long-term vision

Many goal-setting exercises fail to start with a vision. Start here. Think of a huge goal, or a vision for yourself, that aligns with your values. The values must personify who you are, who you want to be and what you stand for. This goal or vision lies in the background and directs our smaller goals. Even when you aren't thinking about your smaller goals, your vision will subconsciously drive your decisions and motivation.

For this exercise, we'll use a common vision in our clubs: becoming a black belt. This can take seven to ten years for many students to achieve.

Step two: Create big goals

Each big goal should have a time frame of twelve to eighteen months. It should take a considerable amount of hard work to achieve. Usually, to achieve big goals you'll need to change your daily habits and work towards many smaller goals (one to three months each). Look at the black belt journey shown at the end of this exercise. From this, we can see the stages are excellent examples of big goals: junior, senior, advanced, black belt and instructor – all typically twelve to eighteen months apart.

Step three: Break down the big goals

We are looking for three- to six-month goals here. These goals must represent a big change in your development. At the Warrior Academy we hold gradings every three to six months, and these provide an excellent step towards a big goal. For example, your goal might be to achieve the next belt – perhaps yellow belt or blue belt.

Step four: Set small goals

What will it take to achieve your three- to six-month goal? To achieve your next belt, you may need to conquer several aspects of your training and get out of your comfort zone a little. We break this down by awarding 'stripes' on our students' belts that represent different parts of their training. Once a student has achieved all five stripes, they're ready for their grading.

Yellow – Leadership (leading the class)

Red – Self-defence

Purple – Fitness

Green – Technique and line work

Black – Sparring

These small steps make a big difference to breaking down those larger goals that can seem so far away. They help to guide you through the goal-setting process.

Step five: Create daily habits

Your daily habits are the smallest of your goals, but gradually they help you achieve your big goals. Plan a positive, productive day. What would the perfect day look like? Who can you help in your day? As a student, can you help your parents at home? For example, you could do this by making your bed each day. Then, look at the small drills you can do at home to help you achieve your small goals. For example, if your small goal is to achieve your fitness stripe, doing push ups and squat jumps every morning and evening will make a difference to you achieving that goal.

Step six: Evaluate your goals

Going through each of the above steps, break down what the result would mean to you. Be as descriptive as possible – how would it make you feel? Developing this understanding will create a deep sense of pride when you achieve the goals you have set. It will also connect you to your true vision.

Step seven: Plan your rewards

This step is like sprinkling motivation over each of the goals we have listed above. By this stage, you have an emotional connection to the goals you are setting. You understand how they will benefit your life.

Step eight: Be accountable

Accountability is vital to keep up on track. We're much more productive when we have someone else to answer to. Having instructors, friends or parents checking in with us from time to time can make a massive difference here. You can create accountability by printing out the above goals and ticking them off each day, week and month. Keep old copies of these goals to motivate you when you plan your next goals.

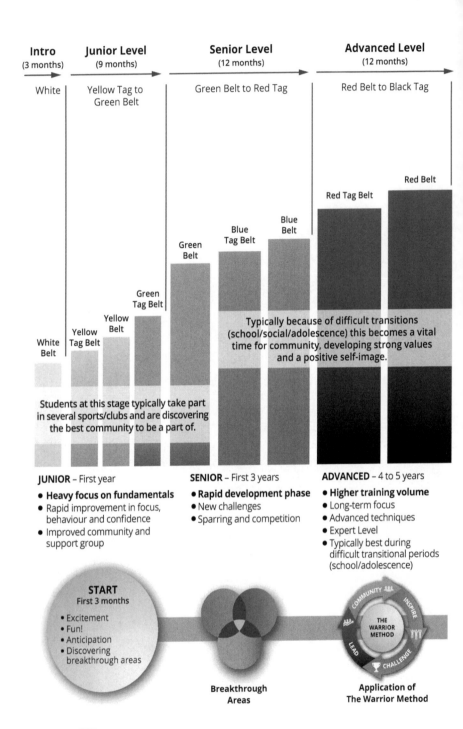

Intro (3 months) → **Junior Level** (9 months) → **Senior Level** (12 months) → **Advanced Level** (12 months)

White | Yellow Tag to Green Belt | Green Belt to Red Tag | Red Belt to Black Tag

White Belt | Yellow Tag Belt | Yellow Belt | Green Tag Belt | Green Belt | Blue Tag Belt | Blue Belt | Red Tag Belt | Red Belt

Typically because of difficult transitions (school/social/adolescence) this becomes a vital time for community, developing strong values and a positive self-image.

Students at this stage typically take part in several sports/clubs and are discovering the best community to be a part of.

JUNIOR – First year
- **Heavy focus on fundamentals**
- Rapid improvement in focus, behaviour and confidence
- Improved community and support group

SENIOR – First 3 years
- **Rapid development phase**
- New challenges
- Sparring and competition

ADVANCED – 4 to 5 years
- **Higher training volume**
- Long-term focus
- Advanced techniques
- Expert Level
- Typically best during difficult transitional periods (school/adolescence)

START First 3 months
- Excitement
- Fun!
- Anticipation
- Discovering breakthrough areas

Breakthrough Areas

COMMUNITY · INSPIRE · THE WARRIOR METHOD · LEAD · CHALLENGE

Application of The Warrior Method

Black Belt Level
(12 months)

Instructor Level
(24 months)

Black Belt to 1st Degree
Assistant Instructor

1st Degree to 2nd Degree
Full Instructor

Black Tag Belt

Junior Black Belt

Assistant Instructor

1st Degree

2nd Degree

Preparation for adult life, success and increasing opportunity with practical skills in leadership, conduct, public speaking and presentation.

BLACK BELT – 5 to 7 years

- **Constant challenges**
- Total focus
- Limitless mindset
- Leadership role
- A long-term development vision required

INSTRUCTOR – 7 to 9 years

- **Mastery of Technique and style**
- Deep Understanding of theory and application
- Dedication and devotion to the Arts
- Development of adult/practical skills
- Vastly increased opportunity

**Black Belt
Character**

185

Black belt journey

Each of the eight steps of the Warrior Academy goal-setting system is built into the black belt journey.

The Warrior Academy daily habits system

Daily habits can put us in a positive mindset for the whole day. I believe a strict routine can yield powerful results for young students. Starting each day in a positive mindset will help. To truly benefit from the goal-setting steps above, we must plan daily habits. This is something we encourage students to do each day.

We focus on connecting the three main things that make up the black belt character:

- Confidence

- Concentration

- Conduct

We ask our students, with our help, to break each of these areas into small tasks. This builds a routine that they can do each day. It should be easy to remember and easy to achieve – ideally, in under five minutes. Any longer and it's unlikely that they'll stick to the routine.

Confidence. One of the best ways to wake up and feel confident, ready to go about our day in a decisive manner with our head held high, is to do some physical exercise. For many of our students, doing a set of ten to fifty press-ups as soon as they wake up does two things. It helps prepare them for their assessments in the Warrior Academy classes and it 'wakes up them', gets the blood pumping and makes them feel fresh and active.

Concentration. We ask our students to do two simple things to improve their concentration at home: make the bed and meditate. These simple tasks lead to brilliant results. By making their bed, students feel organised. It may feel like a mundane task that serves little purpose other than to make their parents happy, but being in an organised, tidy and calm environment helps them concentrate. Students leave their room already feeling a sense of achievement. Students also spend two or three minutes meditating each morning, sitting with their eyes closed and focusing on their breathing, just as they are taught in class. These few moments of pausing will stop their minds from going straight into a busy day, giving them a chance to evaluate their values.

Conduct. One of the best ways to improve a person's mindset and behaviour is to make them aware of how fortunate they are, whatever their situation. We ask students to write down each morning three things they are grateful for. This can be something as simple as sleeping on a comfy bed, having breakfast ready for them or being part of an awesome community. The list grows as students build this daily habit, and the result is an overwhelming feeling of gratitude. This decreases anxiety and boosts happiness. We then ask students to think of one thing they can do in the morning to make someone else happy. Students often choose to clear the table after breakfast or help their brothers or sisters get ready for school.

I'm amazed by the effect that the Warrior Academy daily habits has had on our students, and I encourage you to give it a go at home.

Mentoring your child to set and achieve goals

I've spent years teaching thousands of young people to set and achieve goals. I've found that this process is best achieved by going through each level of the five-level system I have developed.

- Level one: Lay the foundations

- Level two: Initiate opportunities for challenge and adventure

- Level three: Feel, understand and control emotions

- Level four: Provide positive reinforcement

- Level five: Set goals

Level one: Lay the foundations

For a child to truly develop and consider taking on more risk, challenge and adventure, there must be a foundation of unconditional love.

> 'Give the ones you love wings to fly, roots to come back and reasons to stay.'
> — *Dalai Lama*

Unconditional love is the roots. Confidence is the wings. Young people who have both live bigger lives.

Consider the love your child feels from their peers, too. Could your child's peer group be more supportive and positive? Use the community assessment guide provided in chapter four to decide whether your child's communities are a positive or negative influence. Consider the effect your child's peer group will have on their long-term development and their 'inner voice' – how they react to challenges, mistakes, failures and successes. Who we surround ourselves by is an important aspect of our development.

CHALLENGE

Seek out a more positive peer group for your child. Look for a community outside school that has a strong ethos and whose values are aligned with your own.

Level two: Initiate opportunities for challenge and adventure

As parents, we often want to jump in and prevent our children from making a mistake. It's a tough call – we know we can help them, but we also know by doing so we prevent them from learning how to deal with a certain situation.

As I mentioned in the section on stepping back, if you always jump in to save your child they will lack confidence in their ability to overcome a difficult situation or solve a problem. Be their safety net, but give them the space to learn. Competence cultivates confidence. Providing your child with the opportunity to take healthy risks means they will develop independence and pride. They will build strength by making decisions, making mistakes and overcoming defeat and obstacles.

CHALLENGE

Sit down with your child and talk about what they enjoy doing – perhaps a sport, an activity or a class. Talk about who they admire. Who is brilliant at this class, sport or activity, and what makes them great at it? Seek out something achievable from your child's words and talk about how they could achieve it. Challenge your child to achieve the goal and set a time frame.

Level three: Feel, understand and control emotions

When we make a leap out of our comfort zone (for example, by putting our hand up in school to answer a question, entering a public speaking contest or competing in a martial arts competition), we feel anxiety and fear. Fear, the process of feeling fear and the emotions behind it follow a simple process. This process can be learned, understood and controlled, as discussed in chapter 8.

> 'I learned that courage is not the absence of fear but the triumph over it. The brave man is not he who does not feel afraid, but he who conquers that fear.'
> — *Nelson Mandela*

Teach your child not to be worried about the emotions fear brings – they are part of normal life and to feel them is natural. Help your child to understand why they are feeling fear, where it comes from and what to do with their feelings. Learning how to channel their emotional energy so that fear becomes courage, and how to rationalise their emotions to find something positive, will have a profound effect on their confidence. By tackling fear every day, your child's comfort zone will grow and they will make decisions based on a more confident, positive inner voice.

CHALLENGE

Have an open conversation with your child about fear when they next present the symptoms. While doing so, ask your child the two questions below. Be sure to respond to their answer by relating it to your own experiences. This will help to encourage them to share and to feel less isolated.

Question 1: What is making you feel [sad/angry/scared/upset]?

Response: I felt exactly the same thing when I [insert your personal story]. It's actually really normal to feel these things when we are scared or fearful, so you and I are the same.

Question 2: Do you want to know how I dealt with that fear?

Response: I made a list of all the things that could go wrong with what I was doing and then, looking at them on paper, they suddenly didn't feel so scary. I then wrote a list of all the great things that would happen if I completed the challenge, and instead of feeling scared I felt excited about achieving something new!

Remind your child that you will always be there for them, no matter what happens, but that they will feel a huge sense of pride if they conquer what is making them fearful. Depending on the age of the child, you can even give their fear a silly name. This personifies the fear so your child can see it as something separate from themselves. When used with other techniques, I've seen this make a big difference to a child's confidence in tackling fear.

Level four: Provide positive reinforcement

Positive reinforcement is a reward for a positive action or behaviour. With that in mind, it may seem logical that negative reinforcement is a punishment, but this is not the case. Negative reinforcement is the absence of a reward for a behaviour or action.

For the best results, both positive and negative reinforcement should be used alongside each other. Positive reinforcement is the **best** tool for long-term development; over time negative reinforcement loses its power entirely. You can use negative reinforcement to give your child the 'push' we all need at times. This concept of 'push/pull', using both positive and negative reinforcement, is vital to maintaining the perseverance and energy levels needed for challenges and action.

CHALLENGE

Can you think of any challenges your child may be facing? Try to write a list of what you feel would be a suitable reward or positive reinforcement for your child and see if introducing them provides motivation.

Level five: Set goals

The final stage is to set goals. This stage can only be reached once you have successfully completed the other stages because the previous levels build on one another to ensure your child is sufficiently motivated and understands the process of setting goals.

CHALLENGE

Sitting with your child, talk about an upcoming goal and try to plan a reward if they achieve it. Now they are motivated, you can set in motion the first steps of achieving this goal.

Let's wrap it up

In this chapter we have discussed the importance of setting goals, examining the eight-step Warrior Academy goal-setting system in detail.

We have explored the black belt journey and how it provides students with a clear vision and a long-term goal, and we have considered the daily habits system that we teach our students at the Warrior Academy, focusing on the three Cs of confidence, concentration and conduct.

Finally, we have concluded with a five-level process to ensure your child is ready to set and achieve their own goals.

PART FIVE

THE WARRIOR METHOD – LEAD

CHAPTER ELEVEN

Lead

Lead is the last step of the Warrior Method. It comes at the end of our process for developing character, after community, inspire and challenge. Learning to lead is a vital part of my methodology: it prepares students for adult life while solidifying their skills. It gives them pride in their work and ability, a deeper understanding of the processes they have learnt, and a big boost to their confidence.

Why we develop leadership skills

The *Oxford Dictionary of English* defines leadership as 'the action of leading a group of people or an organisation'.

The ability to lead is far more important than we may imagine. In the adult world, leadership is considered a vital skill in management and for the progression of our work life. It's a desired skill for teamwork, too. Leadership is an ability that involves social influence, where the aim is to achieve a specific outcome for a group or organisation. Nurturing leadership skills and qualities from a young age can be hugely beneficial to the development of a child's character and their continued success, opportunity and happiness.

We use leadership skills in many areas of our lives without realising – in the way we communicate and reason with others, in how we motivate ourselves, in our pursuit of challenges and adventure, in how we negotiate, in being reliable, in making decisions and even as part of our emotional intelligence and our ability to forge strong relationships. As we can see, there's far more to leadership than being in management in the adult world. Developing excellent leadership skills builds a strong character. I believe martial arts provide the perfect framework for a child to develop leadership skills in a progressive way.

The benefits of developing leadership skills

Teaching leadership skills from a young age is an incredibly powerful tool for character development. I'll focus on ten important ways that learning leadership skills improves a young person's character at a vital time in their development, before they reach adulthood.

1. Giving your child a sense of responsibility and reliability

When we have a strong sense of responsibility and a record of being responsible, we become reliable. Reliability is an especially important value as we become adults and the outcomes of our tasks and duties are more important or have a larger effect on a wider group of people. From work life to home life, reliability and responsibility are vital.

For many parents, instilling a sense of responsibility in their children is a tough one to crack. We might notice other children doing tasks to help at home without lots of reminding, and wonder why they are able to do this.

It's important to remember that responsibility isn't just about completing a task. Karen Ruskin, author of *The 9 Key Techniques For Raising Respectful Children Who Make Responsible Choices*, says, 'Ingraining responsibility in children is not a trick, but is simply teaching them life skills ... Kids who do not have responsibilities feel entitled and think the world will always do for them.' Alex Barzvi, co-host of the American programme *About Our Kids* on Doctor Radio, says, 'It's also about an attitude, the idea of taking action and being proud of doing it, not just always having your mom and dad do it for you.'

Young people can be taught responsibility through developing their leadership skills. When somebody is acting as a leader, the end result of a task or challenge becomes their responsibility. This pressure to achieve a result or outcome gives the leader a sense of responsibility. A leader is directly responsible for how the team works and performs, and this pressure of accountability improves their performance. If it is framed correctly, young people feel immensely positive about and motivated by their experience as a leader. They enjoy the competitiveness and responsibility involved in aiming for a desired outcome.

Starting young is important. Throwing responsibility at a teenager will be a tough transition – it's a skill and quality that needs to be nurtured from a young age. Teaching leadership skills lays a strong foundation for teaching responsibility before children become teenagers, and before they move into adult life where responsibility is so vital to their success and happiness.

Martial arts develops responsibility because students are expected to work on their individual techniques and exercises to meet regular targets. To develop leadership, students are given teaching roles where they must achieve a specific outcome.

2. Teaching valuable teamwork skills

Teamwork is another vital skill that we develop from a young age. It's a skill that requires us to work co-operatively with others in a group towards a shared goal or purpose that benefits everyone in the team.

Throughout life, we find ourselves working in teams. As adults, we do so at work and in our profession. When we're younger, we work in teams in clubs, classes and sports, and even through play. In each situation, we're much more likely to perform well when we work effectively as a team. This is because excellent teamwork creates synergy – where the combined effect of the team is far greater than the sum of each individual's efforts.

Working as part of a team will strengthen your child's social and emotional skills, help develop their communication skills, and improve their confidence. This all goes a long way to developing their character. By leading a team, we learn to understand what motivates each member of the team, how to motivate others and how to set and achieve goals. It gives us the ability to inspire other people. At the same time, it teaches us valuable lessons about getting the best out of each person's unique skills and personality traits so that everyone works together harmoniously.

Even though martial arts is thought of as an individual sport, where the goal is self-development, they do develop teamwork. Students are expected to inspire their partners, motivating them to continue through tough times. They work as part of a team to ensure they progress – the goals we set are often personal, but students can achieve them more quickly by working as part of a team.

3. Self-motivation and pride

By providing an environment where a child can develop passion and self-motivation, they will become proactive about setting goals and looking for new skills to develop. To develop their leadership qualities, students often have to motivate others, and for this to happen they must be motivated themselves.

If we are given a role of leadership from a young age, we develop a strong sense of who we are, along with great pride in ourselves and our work. This feeling of pride and self-respect stays with us as we grow and develop into adults. It shines through in our attitude to and motivation for new challenges and tasks, and it gives us a strong vision of our future selves.

Through teaching others in martial arts, students develop a sense of pride in their achievements. At some point on their journey, each student is encouraged to pass on their learning to their peers or junior grades. They are motivated to make a difference and to pass on their knowledge, and they enjoy the feelings of

respect and pride that they experience through per-
forming these mini-leadership roles.

4. Ability to reason and negotiate

Part of being a leader is learning to reason and negotiate. This stems not only from having to encourage
and motivate others in our team but also from dealing with emergencies, problems, mistakes, stress and
deadlines. A good leader is able to negotiate a positive, win-win situation that benefits everyone in the
group. In adult life, negotiation and reasoning skills
are used often in work, relationships and our personal life.

In a martial arts context, we teach students to negotiate group dynamics and social settings through our
leadership exercises. This teaches our students to deal
with conflicts and make tough decisions. Students
usually take it in turns to lead a group on a fitness
circuit, through an exercise or on a drill.

5. Resilience and the pursuit of challenge and adventure

Part of being a leader is setting goals. That means having vision and then motivating a group to achieve the
goals set and surpass their expectations. While developing these leadership skills, we begin to understand
the benefits of conquering challenges. This leads us to
pursue challenge and adventure. Challenge becomes

a positive learning experience, so we are driven to complete more challenges.

By seeking out more challenges and adventure, we broaden our comfort zone and become more resilient. We become more able to persevere through difficult times and deal with a greater workload. By developing a strong, resilient mindset that pursues challenge and adventure, we learn to solve bigger problems when they are presented to us – in fact, we seek out bigger problems to solve. As a result, we are able to make a greater impact on our own lives, our community and the world. In martial arts students are consistently encouraged to pursue challenge and adventure by setting goals and stepping out of their comfort zone.

6. Communication, interpersonal skills and emotional intelligence

One of the greatest benefits of developing leadership skills is understanding how to communicate, empathise and understand other people. This gives us a higher emotional intelligence.

The *Oxford Dictionary of English* defines emotional intelligence as 'the capacity to be aware of, control, and express one's emotions, and to handle interpersonal relationships judiciously and empathetically.' As leaders it's vital to be aware of our own and other people's emotions to be able to work effectively as a group towards a desired outcome. Emotional intelligence is an incredibly important part of life, especially as we get older. A person with a high emotional intelligence will have the following attributes:

Self-awareness: The person is aware of their own abilities, strengths and weaknesses, and how their actions affect others. They are also far better at receiving constructive criticism and improving.

Self-regulation: A person with a high emotional IQ (or EQ – emotional quotient) can reveal their emotions in a mature way. This prevents them from holding onto feelings that can cause problems; instead, these feelings are expressed with control.

High motivation: A person with a high EQ tends to have a good level of self-motivation and is able to motivate others. This quality will help them through difficult times and make them optimistic and resilient. They typically have a lot of ambition, which represents itself in how they approach challenges and respond to disappointments.

Empathetic: A person with a high EQ has high levels of compassion and understanding for other people. The ability to understand others is a vital part of being a leader. This quality helps us build relationships throughout our lives.

Interpersonal skills: A person with good interpersonal skills has the ability to build rapport and trust quickly with others in a team. This is a quality that helps us to be part of a positive community and be an influencer. Being a leader means communicating well with your team, and this leadership trait comes from developing interpersonal skills. Through our martial arts classes we encourage students to lead others as part of a structured programme. This helps them develop all of their communication, emotional intelligence and interpersonal skills as they learn to motivate others as well as themselves.

7. Attention to detail

Leaders are responsible for spotting potential problems before they happen and solving them quickly. Leaders must have excellent attention to detail to spot these problems. That attention to detail helps us to perfect our performance – in activities and at work – and improves our work ethic.

As adults, we must perform at a higher level, which requires a lot of focus and concentration. In martial arts, as part of developing students' leadership skills we work on attention to detail with our students in class. This helps them critique their own technique and that of their peers in a positive, constructive and respectful way.

8. Creativity and decision making

Creativity makes life more interesting and fulfilling. Being creative feels good. It drives us forward and makes us unique and original as individuals. As Albert Einstein said, 'Creativity is intelligence having fun.'

When leading, we often need to solve problems quickly, in an environment where we don't control many of the variables. This requires high levels of creativity. We may regularly be asked to achieve outcomes that require us to be highly resourceful. Making decisions quickly is an important part of being a leader too. This centres on our confidence, our belief in ourselves and our judgement.

Creativity and decision making are the more advanced skills of leadership. They are developed as students progress within a community where leadership is engrained in the syllabus, such as our martial arts programme. As the pressure and level of responsibility increase, this motivates students to respond to situations in a professional, creative and decisive way.

9. Conflict resolution

A great leader has the ability to resolve conflict in a group with apparent ease. When a group is under pressure to meet an upcoming deadline or to achieve a particular result, stress levels can rise. The team members will look to their leader for solutions to any conflict that may be caused by the situation. In a martial arts class, students are taught to handle conflict in a sensible and calm manner, without panicking. This is a vital skill for any leader.

10. Practical adult skills, including public speaking

As the above traits show, focusing on developing leadership skills provides a hugely beneficial learning experience for young people as they grow. One of the reasons we emphasise leadership towards the end of the black belt journey is that it helps students prepare for adult life.

In a leading role, we may often be expected to give instructions or presentations to a large group or audience. This makes a leader an influencer. By developing leadership skills, we are directly working on our public speaking skills, including:

- Eye contact
- Voice projection
- How fast we speak
- Body language
- The way we present ourselves professionally

Within our martial arts programme students are encouraged to teach at the front of the class. They are taught that their presentation is important and they must wear their uniform in the correct way. We teach them how to articulate their messages and commands to large groups of students with clarity. This approach helps improve their public speaking skills and prepares them for the adult world.

How martial arts develops leaders in the dojo

Through our martial arts programme, we aim to cultivate excellent leadership skills in our community. As mentioned previously, these skills do far more than teach our children to lead others. They encourage independence in our young students by teaching them about being responsible, being reliable, why attention to detail is important and having pride in their work. Teaching students to lead solidifies their learning and develops important social, public speaking and presentation skills, all of which they can use in their adult lives.

It's important to develop leadership qualities in our young students to give them a head start as adults. Here's how we provide structure to developing leadership qualities.

1. Surround our students with leaders

One of the best ways to encourage students to develop leadership skills is to give everyone a chance to lead. In a typical class of twenty students, we split the class up into smaller groups. In turn, we then build up each student's confidence in teaching a technique. This can start from something as small as a student counting from one to ten in their mini-group, and build up to them teaching a whole class. We take away the pressure of 'leading' by making it an ordinary learning tool and a routine process.

2. Inspire through positive role models

An important aim of our programme is to inspire our students. To do this, we lead by example, proving to students that they can perform at a high level. We encourage young people to challenge themselves and solve bigger problems.

Our instructors all live by a strong moral code. We teach martial arts full time and are incredibly passionate about what we do. We live disciplined lives with a focus on setting and achieving goals and we work closely with our local communities and charities. In our actions and our behaviour, we ensure we are the best possible role models for our students.

3. Line work and belt structure

When I say 'lines' I mean how we line up in class – essentially, in rows of students. In a class of twenty, this may be four rows of five students, for example. Students form their lines in belt order, with the highest grades at the front. This means that when students look in front of them, they see the higher grades. As students go up a belt, they move into the next line. In doing so, they physically become the leaders, ready to help the line of less experienced students behind them.

We split the classes by groups of belts: juniors – first four belts; seniors – next four belts; advanced – final four belts. I've found that by doing this, the students progress more quickly from novice to advanced in their smaller groups. This boosts their confidence and gives them a feeling of responsibility and pride that improves their leadership skills.

4. Imitation

In the early stages, with nervous students we build their confidence in leading by asking them to imitate their instructor. An example of this is asking them to repeat what we are saying as a group and then as individuals, for example, 'Why do we bow?' generates the set response, 'To show respect', which gets them used to being vocal in a group of peers and slowly builds their confidence. Once they are comfortable with this, we can start giving them more responsibility in class as a leader, including standing at the front of class to show a technique or taking a class through a combination. This has a rapid effect on the development of their confidence and their leadership skills.

5. Placing a high value on perseverance

We make sure students understand and highly value the trait of perseverance. In class, we tell stories about students who have had a tough time but have kept going to achieve great things. We tell stories about leaders who transformed their students' lives, and we talk about our own experiences of facing up to adversity and overcoming problems with perseverance and a black belt mindset. These stories go a long way to reinforcing the value of never giving up – part of the core mindset of a leader.

6. Placing a high value on integrity and accountability

Integrity and accountability are important traits in a leader. We ensure that students understand the value of integrity and how to show this in their day-to-day lives. We hold regular talks where we discuss being true to ourselves and holding ourselves accountable. Because in martial arts the focus is on self-development, each student is responsible for their own progress. This means that these values are reinforced regularly.

Here's an insight from a parent into how the programme develops maturity and emotional intelligence.

When Joe was about three we realised that he was struggling socially. He was unable to cope with change, his language was severely delayed and his emotional self-regulation was inconsistent. He had been a smiley, happy baby and now we could see him losing all sense of self-worth. Over the years we tried many different things and along the way he was diagnosed with Asperger's syndrome. I have lost count of the number of times I have spoken to teachers at the end of a tricky day or spent several hours in the evening talking through the events at school so that he saw where he could have reacted differently.

He has always been excellent at sport, but his downfall has always been to react badly if he has a setback. Any sport he does has to be carefully managed, and team sports can be a particular source of conflict because he does not understand why people are not consistently giving of their best all the time like he is. The rules become a straitjacket for him. Many times, we have seen him not reach his sporting potential because of some minute detail being wrong or him getting obsessed by something unfair.

When he started martial arts with the Warrior Academy in November 2016 I hoped that this would provide the framework for him to respond positively. The clear structure of martial arts and the Warrior values were perfect for him to explore his emotions and to learn about personal responsibility. He found the mindfulness aspect during each class very calming and was able to use this in other aspects of his life when he became stressed. In every class I have seen him in, he presents as someone who is empathetic, interested in others, kind and respectful to both students and staff. The kindness, support and challenge shown to him by the Warrior Academy team has allowed him to develop a really strong sense of self-worth and a desire to push himself.

He is now in Year 6 and is a member of the school council, on the Worship Committee and identified by school staff as the most changed member of his year group. 'A different child from his earlier self,' says his current teacher. He is also looked up to as a role model by fellow students and I am regularly stopped by parents and grandparents to be told how polite and naturally helpful he is. At his last competition he coached his best friend through his weapons routine, even though he was competing for the same trophy.

I am unbelievably proud of how he has developed and what he has become. Martial arts has played a huge part in that along with the love and care from the whole Warrior Academy team. Recently he was chosen to represent the Warrior Academy at the English National Tae Kwon Do Championships. He was extremely stressed by the responsibility of it all, but with the support of Seb and Matt he made it through the day and despite setbacks on the day was comfortable enough to react positively and learn from the experience.

Being his mum is a constant source of joy and I am really proud of all he has and will achieve. Martial arts has allowed him to be the best he can possibly be.

Rachael, parent of a Warrior Academy student

Our '10 Skills' programme

To prepare our students for leadership in adult life, we created a 10 Skills programme.

We run the programme with small groups of between two and four students, usually with each student receiving one-to-one mentoring from one of our instructors. We guide students through each leadership skill. As they learn to evaluate where their strengths and weaknesses lie, we work with them to develop each skill. The programme focuses on the following ten skills.

1. **Passion**: A visible passion that enables you to motivate others.

2. **Communication**: Effective communication between peers and the team.

3. **Experience**: A true leader has experience they can relate to their team.

4. **Delegation**: The ability to use your team effectively and give each member a role.

5. **Mindset**: A strong mindset, a desire to succeed and the ability to influence.

6. **Reliability and responsibility**: Qualities that are needed to achieve your goals.

7. **Creativity and flexibility**: These qualities enable you to think quickly and find creative solutions.

8. **Presentation**: Body language, appearance and public speaking.

9. **Conduct**: A black belt leader lives by a moral code that includes integrity and courtesy.

10. **Attention to detail**: High levels of focus and excellent attention to detail.

Developing leadership skills at home

I've talked about how developing young people's leadership skills can have a hugely positive and long-lasting effect as they grow into adults. Even without a leadership or character-development programme, you can make a lasting impact on your child by developing leadership skills at home. There are four effective things you can do at home to encourage your child to become an excellent leader.

1. Encourage an entrepreneurial spirit. By encouraging an entrepreneurial spirit in our children, we spur them on to seek out problems in the world and solve them. You'll see this reflected in their approach to challenges, and eventually it will ensure they have a bigger impact in the community as they grow older.

2. Encourage reading and self-education. A thirst for knowledge is a valuable trait in young people, and it can ensure that they develop quickly into leaders in their chosen sport, skill or subject. A leader often needs to rapidly pick up a new skill or task to ensure they can help others in their group. This ability stems from a passion for learning and self-development, which can be instilled from a young age.

3. Encourage emotional intelligence. By regularly asking our children how their actions may affect other people's feelings, and gearing conversations towards the complexity of human emotions, we will teach them the importance of how they approach and communicate with others. As they begin to understand this, they will improve their interpersonal skills and, in turn, their relationships.

4. Encourage children to blaze their own trail. By encouraging children to make their own decisions after evaluating a situation, we will teach them about responsibility, goal setting and perseverance. This goes hand in hand with encouraging them to be independent and creative. As Madeleine Albright, the former US Secretary of State said, 'Real leadership comes from the nudging of an inner voice. It comes from realizing that the time has come to move beyond wanting to doing.'

Let's wrap it up

In this chapter we have discussed the huge value that developing leadership skills in young students has in preparing them for life. We have introduced martial arts as a natural leadership development tool for parents, given the natural progression within a martial arts community from beginner to leader. We have explored how the Warrior Academy has taken this further with our 10 Essential Skills programme, which has been designed to give our older students a massive head start in life as they become adults.

Finally, we have concluded this chapter with an insight into how I believe we can develop leadership skills at home, in the home dojo.

CONCLUSION

What's Next?

If you are a parent, I hope this book has given you a deeper insight into martial arts as an alternative that can help you develop the character of your children. I hope that by sharing our methodology with you, you may be inspired to find a local martial arts club, wherever you are in the world. Martial arts will help you enrich your child's life so that they go on to live a wonderful and compelling life outside of the dojo.

If you are a teacher, educator or instructor, I hope this book has given you a methodology you can apply to your own classes, courses or clubs to help develop the character of young people and make an impact on many lives. We have had incredible success (supported by the statistics, surveys and case studies from our clubs) by working on each student's breakthrough areas with a strong focus on character development.

We rarely achieve great things alone. It's when we look back that we can join up the dots. Throughout my life I have been blessed with fantastic role models who have given me life-changing support, brilliant communities, inspiration, ambition and drive. These role models have challenged me, encouraged me to pursue adventure, taught me resilience, courage and perseverance, and given me the skills to be an influencer and lead others.

Finally, a little message to our students, who may read this book in the future and look back. Understand that you always will be a martial artist – the arts are a journey for life, and our character is always developing. Always be respectful, share what you have learnt, be bold, inspire others, build communities around strong values, give back to your martial arts community, challenge yourself, get out there and solve big problems in the world … and always remember that courage earns confidence.

References And Further Reading

Bardwick, JM (1995) Danger in the Comfort Zone: From Boardroom to Mailroom – How to break the entitlement habit that's killing American business. Nashville, TN: Amacom. (Kindle edition available)

Barnett, A (2016) 'Children own their first mobile phone aged seven – and browse internet at five', iNews, https://inews.co.uk/news/technology/children-first-mobile-phone-aged-seven-browse-internet-five

Beland, L-P, and Murphy, R (2015) 'Communication: Technology, distraction and student performance', CEP Discussion Paper No 1350, May, London School of Economics/Centre for Economic Performance, http://cep.lse.ac.uk/pubs/download/dp1350.pdf

Brown, B (2010) *The Gifts of Imperfection: Let go of who you think you're supposed to be and embrace who you are*. Center City, MN: Hazelden Foundation.

Daily Express (2008) '"Impersonal" education criticised', *Daily Express*, 18 April, https://express.co.uk/ news/uk/41698/Impersonal-education-criticised

Department for Work and Pensions (2017) National Statistics: Households below average income, 1994/95-2015/16, www.gov.uk/government/statistics/ households-below-average-income-199495-to-201516

Dixon, C (no date) 'The ADHD mindfulness craze: it all started with one little study', MindfullyADD, https://mindfullyadd.com/adhd-mindfulness-craze

Donelly, L (2017) 'Children become less active age just seven', *The Daily Telegraph*, 14 March, https:// telegraph.co.uk/news/2017/03/14/children-become-less-active-age-just-seven-major-study-finds

Gingerbread (2017) Quarterly Labour Force Survey Household Dataset, April-June 2015, http://gingerbread. org.uk/content/365/Statistics

Lightfoot, L (2016) 'Nearly half of England's teachers plan to leave in next five years', *The Guardian*, 22 March, https://theguardian.com/education/2016/mar/22/ teachers-plan-leave-five-years-survey-workload-england

Kemper, AR, et al. (2018) *Attention Deficit Hyperactivity Disorder: Diagnosis and Treatment in Children and Adolescents. Comparative Effectiveness Review* 203, US Agency for Healthcare Research and Quality,

https://effectivehealthcare.ahrq.gov/sites/default/files/pdf/
cer-203-adhd-final_0.pdf

Marketwired (2012) 'Generation Lonely? 39 Percent
of Americans Spend More Time Socializing Online
Than Face-to-Face', www.marketwired.com/press-release/
generation-lonely-39-percent-americans-spend-more-time-
socializing-online-than-face-1648444.htm

NBC News (2014) 'Teens more stressed out
than adults, survey shows', NBC News, 11
February, https://nbcnews.com/health/kids-health/
teens-more-stressed-out-adults-survey-shows-n26921

Office for National Statistics (2014) Marriages
in England and Wales (Provisional):
2012 (statistical bulletin), www.ons.gov.uk/
peoplepopulationandcommunity/birthsdeathsandmarriages/
marriagecohabitationandcivilpartnerships/bulletins/
marriagesinenglandandwalesprovisional/2014-06-11

Office for National Statistics (2017) Families and
households: 2017 (statistical bulletin), www.ons.gov.uk/
peoplepopulationandcommunity/birthsdeathsandmarriages/
families/bulletins/familiesandhouseholds/2017

Office for National Statistics (2017) Working
and workless households in the UK: Apr to
June 2017 (statistical bulletin), www.ons.gov.
uk/employmentandlabourmarket/peopleinwork/
employmentandemployeetypes/bulletins/
workingandworklesshouseholds/apriltojune2017

Pessler, LM, et al. (2011) 'Effects of a restricted elimination diet on the behaviour of children with attention deficit hyperactivity disorder (INCA study): a randomised controlled trial', *The Lancet*, 377(9764), 494–503, https://ncbi.nlm.nih.gov/pubmed/21296237

Psychology Today (no date) 'Adolescence', https://psychologytoday.com/us/basics/adolescence

Qu, Y, et al. (2015) 'Buffering effect of positive parent-child relationships on adolescent risk taking: A longitudinal neuroimaging investigation', *Developmental Cognitive Neuroscience*, October, 15, 26–34, https://ncbi.nlm.nih.gov/pubmed/26342184

Sifferlin, A (2013) 'The most stressed-out generation? Young adults', *Time*, 7 February, *Time*, http://healthland.time.com/2013/02/07/the-most-stressed-out-generation-young-adults

Social Issues Research Centre (2008) *Childhood and Family Life: socio-demographic changes* (report). Oxford: Social Issues Research Centre, www.education.gov.uk/publications/eOrderingDownload/Appendix-G_SIRC-report.pdf

Stomp Out Bullying (no date) 'Why do kids bully?', https://stompoutbullying.org/get-help/about-bullying-and-cyberbullying/why-do-kids-bully

Thompson, C (2005) 'Meet the life hackers', *The New York Times*, 16 October, https://nytimes.com/2005/10/16/magazine/meet-the-life-hackers.html

Tugend, A (2011) 'Tiptoeing out of one's comfort zone (and of course, back in)', *The New York Times*, 11 February, https://nytimes.com/2011/02/12/your-money/12shortcuts.html

The Daily Telegraph (2010) 'One in four socialises more online than in person', *The Daily Telegraph*, 8 November , http://telegraph.co.uk/news/newstopics/howaboutthat/8115578/One-in-four-socialises-more-online-than-in-person.html

The Warrior Academy (2018) 'Warrior Method: Overview', https://warrioracademy.co.uk/overview

Weintraub, P (2014) 'Connecting ADHD and nutrition', Experience Life, https://experiencelife.com/article/connecting-adhd-and-nutrition

Acknowledgements

It takes a village to raise a warrior… and I have a great team who raise hundreds of warriors across the UK. Nothing great is ever achieved alone and so I have a lot of thanks to give. To my amazing fiancée and incredible mother of our daughter, who constantly keeps me in the moment and reminds me of what's truly important in my life. Without your support, I would not be able to build a family and pursue my dreams; with your support we can achieve both – thank you.

To my father, the greatest mentor, influencer and role model I could have wished for. You have taught me the importance of character and that life should be an incredible adventure, filled with opportunity. Now I pass that message on to my own children – thank you.

To my mother, a constant support and caring influence in my life. You have always been there to help me through the most difficult of times, teaching me the real meaning of emotional intelligence – thank you.

To the incredible Warrior Academy team: passionate, dedicated instructors and admin staff who constantly go above and beyond the call of duty to give the very best to students and colleagues. You inspire me every day with your work ethic, attention to detail, dedication to martial arts, your patience – and often your sense of humour; this makes this journey so rewarding. Thank you all; we are transforming young lives.

To the Warrior Academy parents and ambassadors: you have placed your trust in us to help you develop the character of your children. Without your support nothing is possible and with your support we believe your child will go on to live an exciting and compelling life outside of the dojo. I'm constantly blown away by the support our Warrior parents show us. Thank you all for being part of our community for so many years, for contributing to this book, for sending in your stories – and for your honesty and sincerity.

To my fantastic martial arts senseis, Krus, mentors and instructors around the world, including Michael Tucker, Michael Massie, Kru Ped and Salvatore Pace. You have all been an inspiration in my life and guided my path through martial arts. Thank you.

The Author

Sebastian is the founder and head instructor of the Warrior Academy. In eight years the Warrior Academy has grown to over 45 clubs, and now over a thousand students go through the programme each year. It  has become one of the most successful independent martial arts schools in the UK.

Sebastian has spent twenty years studying six different martial arts around the world. He has won several national UK titles (British Champion, English Champion and West of England Champion) and trained and competed professionally for over eighteen months in full-contact Muay Thai in intense Thai boxing camps.

Sebastian's passion for combining adventure, extreme challenges and self-development has taken him on more than five hundred skydives and base jumps, including wingsuit base-jumping off some of the most beautiful mountains in the world. He has travelled across the Sahara Desert on a mountain bike, motor-biked across Vietnam and trained to become a pilot.

Sebastian believes passionately that martial arts is an empowering self-development tool that should be in every parent's arsenal. A high-quality martial arts programme will improve your child's behaviour at home, which will lower your stress and improve your family time.

Contact details

www.facebook.com/TheWarriorAcademyLTD

www.instagram.com/warrior_academy/

www.twitter.com/warrioracad

Printed in Great Britain
by Amazon